LOGISTICS MANAGEMENT

LOGISTICS MANAGEMENT

By

Dr. Shardul Chaubey

Senior Lecturer

School of Management Sciences

Varanasi

DPH

DISCOVERY PUBLISHING HOUSE PVT. LTD.

NEW DELHI-110 002

PPublished by:
Namit Wasan
DISCOVERY PUBLISHING HOUSE PVT. LTD.
4383/4B, Ansari Road, Darya Ganj
New Delhi-110 002 (India)
Phone : +91-11-23279245; 23253475; 43596065
E-mail : discoverybooksindia@gmail.com
discoverypublishinghouse@gmail.com
namitwasan9@gmail.com
web : www.discoverypublishinggroup.com

First Edition: **2011**
ISBN: 978-81-8356-794-7

Logistics Management

Preface

'Logistics Management' is increasingly becoming a topic of interest among academicians and practitioners since it may lead to reduced operational costs, improved delivery performance and increased customer satisfaction levels. The logistics market in India alone is estimated to be $ 97 billion at the micro level each manufacturing and marketing companies spend nearly 5-35 per cent of sales on logistics. Transportation, handling warehousing and inventory carrying are major cost components. Improvement in logistics gets reflected in reduction in inventory levels short delivery schedules and improved servicing standards. Most of the companies providing logistics services in India use traditional technologies, considering the vast potential in the field of logistics government of India approached business boom in the country so it created Container Corporation of India separating it from Indian Railways. With the use of containers, it changed and facilitated business activity in India through its terminals. Use of Containers and Information Technologies have fastened the pace of trade and improved logistics management practices in India. Container Corporation of India is one of the company in India which is considered as a symbol of growth. To know its practices and working it needs study as container has become the most sought after mode of cargo movement in the field of logistics.

The study has been divided into nine chapters. The *first* chapter deals with the concept and evolution of logistics management. The *second* chapter deals with the logistics management practices in India where some practices on Amul, Mumbai Dabawallah has been taken up. In the *third* chapter research methodology has been discussed. The *fourth* chapter deals the bases of Container Corporation of India (CONCOR). In this chapter conceptual framework of containerisation, its evolution and types, warehousing, transportation and multimodal transportation has been discussed in detail. The *fifth* chapter is on Container Corporation and its practices. This chapter deals with present arena of significance and working of CONCOR. It depicts that how CONCOR organisation structure facilitates domestic and international trade through its container freight stations and inland container depots existing in the country. The *sixth* chapter deals the marketing functions of CONCOR. Marketing aspect like transportation services of container through terminals, need of industrial marketing, export and import trade and four *Ps* of marketing are being dealt in the chapter. The *seventh* chapter is on the tenets of financial of CONCOR. For the purpose an in-depth financial analysis has been undertaken on the basis of six years annual report of CONCOR. This chapter includes the detailed financial analysis like ratio analysis, cash flow analysis. The *eighth* chapter is on Human Resource function of CONCOR. Human resource management practices of CONCOR has been dealt including Human resource philosophies and believes practices in CONCOR, recruitment and selection policies, compensation policy etc. The *ninth* chapter is the crux of the study. Findings and suggestions have been given in the last chapter.

Logistics Management (LM) practices in India are improving and it is assisting international and national business to grow at a rapid pace. The emergence of new technologies is becoming driver and facilitator of this industry. This study tells about the concept and what kind of practices is being followed in Logistics Industry. This might help the major industry in understanding the practices and its utility in the movement of cargo, multi modal transportation, warehousing facility, and containerisation process through ICD and CFS.

The concept of logistics management is at evolving stage and various new dimensions are being added to this at a regular pace. The work has brought out the latest developments taking place in the area of international and national trade through containerisation.

The present study is constrained to limit its scope to the currently available information. The logistics industry is going through the phase of restructuring as it is difficult to visualise at this moment the final shape of the whole picture. The study being restricted to one company, it does not make any attempt to generalise the outcome of the study for the industry as whole.

SHARDUL CHAUBEY

Acknowledgements

On the verge of completion of this study, I take this opportunity to express my sincere and worthy feelings to express the overwhelming sense of gratitude and regard to all those who made this work possible.

I express my deep sense of gratitude to my guide Dr. Sudhir Kumar Shukla, Reader, Department of Commerce, Mahatma Gandhi Kashi Vidhyapith, for his supervision and guidance. He has been a perfect and ideal guide and has been a consistent source of inspiration and motivation throughout the work. It is being said that goal can only be achieved when a proper direction and guidance is given. I have been fortunate enough to have a guide who not only guided me but also shared my tense moment.

I also offer my regards to Prof. M. B Shukla. Dean, Faculty of Commerce and Management for his valuable suggestion on this topic. I also express my gratitude to Dr. Ashok Kumar Mishra, Head, Department of Commerce and other faculty members of Faculty of Commerce, Mahatma Gandhi Kashi Vidhyapith; Varanasi for their support and encouragement.

Since this research is the outcome of the consistent interaction with officials of Container Corporation of India, Indian Rail Transport, Inland Container Depots at Tughlakabad, Madhosingh and Haldia Port authorities, I offer my gratitude to all those luminaries from corporate world who have been kind enough to guide me at different stages of the work. I am very grateful to Mr. Nalin Singhal, MD, IRCTC, Mr. S. Roy, Assistant Commissioner of Haldia

Port Trust, Mr. Debjit Mukherjee, Custom Officer, Haldia Port, Mr. K. Batra GM, CONCOR Mr. Rajgopalan, PRO of CONCOR, Mr. Mulgaonkar, ICD Tughlakabad in-charge who spared time from their busy schedule and guided me with their valuable, knowledge, information and suggestions. I offer deep regards to Mr. MK Sengupta, former IAS official and Chairman, International Cargo Management Services, Kolkata, Dr. Arindam Sengupta, former Indian Foreign Service official and Managing Director of International Tour Link Services Kolkata, who not only spare their valuable time from busy schedule but also coordinated and assisted in my endeavour in visiting to restricted sea port area.

I am highly indebted to Dr. M. P. Singh, Executive Secretary of School of Management of Sciences for his kind and valuable support to work. I am also thankful of Prof. PN Jha, Director, School of Management of Sciences for his cooperation during my research work. Words will not be enough to assess assistance given by my colleague Dr. Amit Gautam. My deep sense of gratitude to him. I also offer my sincere thanks to all my colleagues in School of Management Sciences for their encouragement and consistent intellectual support. I also want to extend my thanks to my colleague Mr Shyam Lal Dev Pandey and GBS Jauhari for being a constant source of encouragement.

I also thank my friend, Shantanu Tripathi and brother-in-law Siddharth who accompanied and shared tense moments.

Last but not the least is my family, I would like to convey my regards to them. I am and shall always remain indebted to my mother Smt. Shakuntala Sharma, my father Sri Harswaroop Chaubey, brother Sharad Chaubey, my sisters, sister-in-law and brother-in-laws, wife Dr Sangeeta for their affection, cooperation and encouragement.

Shardul Chaubey

Contents

Chapter 1
Introduction to Logistics Management

Wars have been won or lost on the strength of logistics capability or lack of it. Although quite an old concept, logistics has been becoming efficient only since the globalisation wave of the early 1990s and hence, the business supported by it, world-wide, have been pushed for competitive balance sheets, providing consumers a better product /service and yet adding value to its investors.

Triggering intense competition, globalisation, coupled with liberalisation, forced both private and public firms to commit themselves to making available to their customers the right material of right condition, at the right time and place at the lowest cost—be it product or a service. The World Bank, in a recent survey *Connecting to Compete: Trade Logistics in the Global Economy,* has developed a Logistics Performance Index(LPI) that can serve as a benchmarking tool for measuring performance of businesses along a country's logistics supply chain. The Bank study asserts that countries that are able to connect to the global logistics web would not only have access to vast markets but also remain a part of the global trade growth[1]. It also warns that those countries whose links with the global logistics chain are weak are bound to face the large and growing costs of exclusion from international trade.

Since the beginning of the last decade of the twentieth century, there has been a metamorphic environmental transformation in the business world, which resulted into tremendous growth opportunities in one hand, and more complicated business problems threatening to even survival, on the other. Numerous brands of cars and two wheelers, toilet soaps and shampoos, detergent cakes and powders, textiles and garments are available against an at least six years' waiting list for a Bajaj Scooter and premium grade Dalda during a festival period. This is the outcome of heavy industrialisation as a consequence of the government's liberalisation policy, rapid innovations in the field of science and technology along with the emergence of world market as global village.

Apart from the above macro reasons, certain micro reasons are equally responsible for further intrications, like consumers becoming very selective and conscious about their purchase decisions, followed by distributors'/retailers consciousness about their own return on any investment due to the availability of attractive trade opportunities. Hence, in the fiercely global competitive environment as a result of liberalisation, privatisation and globalisation of almost all the economies of the world, it is very important for every organisation to generate the highest level of customer satisfaction, while delivering the highest value to its shareholders. In such an erratic marketplace, companies have to put their best efforts towards formulating market oriented and customer-focussed strategies.

That is why, despite an economic slump in the recent past, companies are increasing their product portfolio, with a focus on quick information, prominent display, ready and intact delivery, 24 hours on the spot after-sales service, eagerness to sort out complaints, etc, in order to satisfy their consumers with a difference. But, for such a set of offering, they have to rely on their marketing intermediaries, because qualitative results of marketing largely depend on the efficient display of marketing acumen of those dealers who have an ultimate interface with end users for a final sales deal. That is why companies are putting in their best efforts to keep their marketing intermediaries happy, loyal and well motivated towards business and trade and have started recognising them as business partners rather than traders. Additionally, to generate the highest value to shareholders, companies need to offer cost-efficient best services, coupled with an improvement of productivity and profitability by means of optimum utilisation of resources, avoiding idle time for any of them. To attain all of the goals, companies have to present best quality product at a reasonably least price as and when required, avoiding a stock-out situation which has given the impetus of Logistics Management, since it has the ability to ensure a consistency in the quality, tremendous cost-saving potential and making available goods at the place of requirements in time.

CONCEPT OF LOGISTICS

Logistics is recent addition in the jargon of integrated business management, formerly with the traditional fields of marketing, finance and production and personnel, although it has been an integral part of these sectors since the Industrial Revolution. Business logistics, physical distribution, materials management outbound logistics, in-bound logistics, logistics management, supply chain management are only some of the terms being used to define and describe the concept of approximately the same subject—logistics, perhaps due to rapid change in the scope and wide use of the subject matter.

Logistics can be defined as *having the right quantity at the right time for the right price.*[2] It is the science of process. Incorporates all industry sectors, and manages the fruition of project life cycles, supply chains and resultant efficiencies. Logistics as a concept is considered to evolve from the military's need to supply themselves as they moved from their base to a forward position. In ancient Greek, Roman and Byzantine empires, there were military officers with the title

'*Logistikas*' who were responsible for financial and supply distribution matters. The Oxford English dictionary defines *logistics* as: *"The branch of military science having to do with procuring, maintaining and transporting material, personnel and facilities.* "In 1905 Major Chauncey B. Baker wrote 'That branch of the Art of War pertaining to the movement and supply of armies is called Logistics'[3].

Logistics systems and various models were used by military forces during World War II to ensure that troops and material made available at the right place to meet the country's requirement. For instance in a book of Gulf War, it is noted on the first phase that US forces planned, moved, and served 122 million meals during the brief engagement—a task comparable to feeding all the residents of Wyoming and Vermonts three meals a day for forty days. Hence from the military point of view, logistics refers to a supportive system which reflects the practical art of moving armies and materials engaged in combats enemy to achieve the desired results. Logistics as its own concept in business evolved only in the 1950s. This was mainly due to the increasing complexity of supplying one's business with materials and shipping out products in an increasingly globalised supply chain, calling for experts in the field.

BUSINESS LOGISTICS

In business, logistics may have either internal focus, or external focus covering the flow from originating supplier to end-user (see supply chain management). The main functions of a logistics manager include purchasing, transport, warehousing, and the organising and planning of these activities. Logistics managers combine a general knowledge of each of these functions so that there is a coordination of resources in an organisation. There are two fundamentally different forms of logistics. One optimises a steady flow of material through a network of transport links and storage nodes. The other coordinates a sequence of resources to carry out some project.

MILITARY LOGISTICS

In military logistics, experts manage how and when to move resources to the places they are needed. In military science, maintaining one's supply lines while disrupting those of the enemy is a crucial—some would say the most crucial element of military strategy, since an armed force without food, fuel and ammunition is defenseless. The Iraq war was a dramatic example of the importance of logistics. It had become very necessary for the US and its allies to move huge amounts of men, materials and equipment over great distances. Logistics was successfully used for this effective movement. The defeat of the British in the American War of Independence, and the defeat of Rommel in World War II, have been largely attributed to logistical failure. The historical leaders Hannibal Barca and Alexander the Great are considered to have been logistical geniuses.

Today, in the industrial and commercial world, logistics has acquired wider meaning. Essentially, it covers activities for the material flow from the source to the processing facilities, and subsequent distribution of finished goods from there to the ultimate users. Previously, the term physical distribution was commonly used, which refers to manufacturing and commerce to describe the broad range of activities concerned with efficient movement of finished products from the end of production line to the consumers. An early definition encompassing the total material flow involves 'a total approach to the management of all activities involved in physically acquiring, moving and storing raw materials, in-process inventory and finished goods inventory from the point of origin to the point of use or consumption' (Lalonde *et al.*, 1970)

In 1961, this same term has been defined as that area of business management responsible for the movement of raw materials and finished products and the development of material system. The Council of Logistics Management (CLM), a prestigious professional organisation, modified its

1976 definition of Physical Distribution Management by first changing the term to Logistics and then changing the definition as follows:

> Logistics is the process of planning, implementing and controlling of efficient, effective flow and storage of goods, services and related information from the point of origin to the point of consumption for the purpose of conforming to consumer expectation.[4]

A more systematic definition of Logistics management has been given by Bowersox and Closs (1996) as: Logistical management includes the design and administration of system to control the flow of materials, work-in-process, and finished inventory to support business unit strategy.

On the basis of above facet of logistics management, a more comprehensive definition of Logistics management is: Logistics management refers to designing, developing, producing and operating an integrated system which responds to customer expectations by making available the required quantity of required quality products as and when required to offer best customer service at the least possible costs. It is an internal integration of interrelated managerial functions to ensure a smooth flow of raw materials from the point of inception to the first production point, semi- finished Goods within production process and finished goods from the last point to the point of consumption.

Hence, a set of activities which are involved in the gamut of logistics include procurement, materials handling, storage and warehousing, protective packaging, order processing, forecasting, inventory management, transportation, and related information system.

After careful analysis and review of various definitions, the major features of logistics management may be drawn as:

(1) It ensures a smooth flow of all types of goods such as raw materials, work-in-process and finished goods;

(2) It has the ability to meet customer expectations and requirements of goods;

(3) It ensures the delivery of quality product;

(4) It offers the best possible customer at the least possible cost;

(5) It is an integration of various managerial functions for optimisation of resources;

(6) It deals with the movement and storage of goods in appropriate quantity;

(7) It enhances productivity and profitability.[5]

EVOLUTION OF THE LOGISTICS CONCEPT

In a broader sense, logistics is seen to have developed as a society transported from the stage of human self sufficiency to the era of exchange which was needed in the socio-economic system. This exchange system had given birth to the concept of trading largely due to division of labour, industrialisation and urbanisation of the population. Logistics now goes on all over the world, twentyfour hours of every day, seven days a week during fiftytwo weeks a year, in every nation, regardless of their political philosophies.

Before the 1950s, no formal theory or concept of logistics existed but the logistical functions were performed in the corporate world without due recognition. The second half of the twentieth century witnessed a phenomenal growth and development in the overall concept and approach towards logistics. Despite significant contribution of logistics during World War II, many of the logistical techniques were ignored temporarily during the post war surge in economic activity and the concentration of business activities were on filling the post-war demands for goods. It was only during the recession of the 1950s, that managers were compelled to examine their physical distribution system. And from there, the discipline of business, logistics has advanced from the warehouse and transportation dock to the boardroom of leading global enterprises.

With the transportation of the business function itself there has been transformation in the concept of logistics, which has been systematically divided into four phases namely:

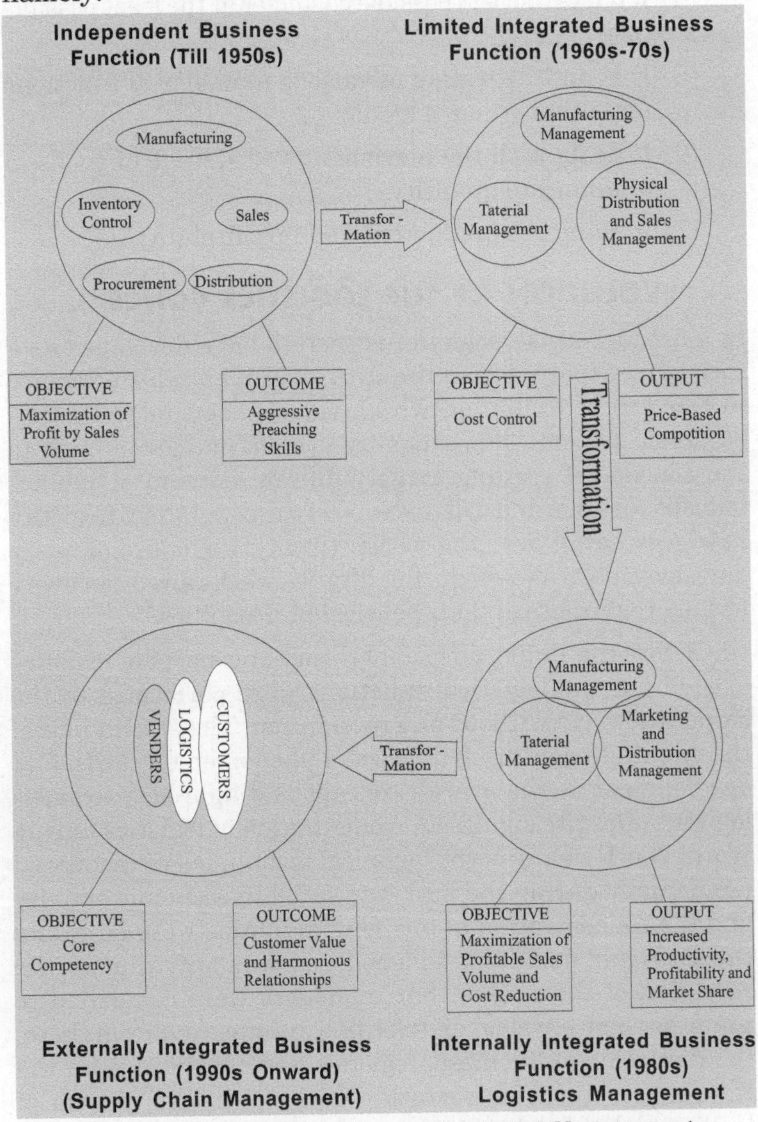

Fig. 1.1. Evolution of the Concept Logistics Management

Independent Business Function Era (Till 1950s)

During the early phase of the industrial growth, emphasis was on the problems of production, mainly due to characteristics of economy of abundance. Companies were under tremendous pressure to increase production capacity due to high demand created by war-time shortages, followed by very limited number of players. That is why the genesis of the various principles of scientific management in the latter part of the nineteenth century and early twentieth century contributed significantly in resolving production problems. In such an environment of technical capacity for mass-production, production led business functions dominated the whole enterprise, which may reflect the managerial mindset of capacity creation, work methods and volume of production and their storage and transportation. Hence in this stage, logistical function was limited only to warehousing and transportation of raw materials and finished goods.[6]

'Furthermore, this era reflected independent business function because each and every function such as procurement of inventory, production, sales and distribution were all independently performed. For instance, the attitude was such that the sales department would sell whatever the plant produced. In other words, the function of sales department was simply to sell by the production and financial managers.

The objective of this stage was to maximise the profit by a corresponding maximisation of sales volume by means of aggressive selling and preaching skills of the sales force. This stage was the phenomena of till the 1950s.

Limited Internally Integrated Business Function Era (1960s-1970s)

With the beginning of the 1960s, corporate enterprises started experiencing difficulties in the marketplace while converting their products into cash, mainly due to three reasons:

(*a*) A large number of new players entering the market resulted into competitive environment;

(*b*) The recession of 1958; and

(*c*) The demand for most of the consumer and infrastructural goods became saturated and resulted into a profit squeeze.

In order to overcome the prevailing competitive environment, corporate enterprises started searching for new tools and techniques for most efficient cost control systems. At the same time, they also realised that physical distribution and logistics were activities that costs had neither been carefully studied nor coordinated. Infact, this era had given a real impetus to the concept of logistics.

Prior to the period of 1960s, activities such as procurement, inventory or raw materials, work-in-process and finished goods, storage and warehousing, traffic and transportation, etc, were performed in a fragmented manner and caused poor performance and high costs. But in this era of functional management during the period of 1960s and 1970s, two limited internally integrated business functions—materials management and physical distribution management were coined in the jargon of business management in addition to traditional functions like finance, personnel, sales, production. The concept of materials management refers to planning, implementation and control of activities responsible for the flow of materials into an organisation. In other words, materials management involves functions like order placement procurement of raw materials, components, and work-in process, their inventory levels, in-bound transportation, storage etc. On the other hand, physical distribution management deals with planning, implementation and control of activities referring to the flow of finished goods from the last point of production to the ultimate users, *i.e.* it included functions like out-bound transportation, protective packaging, distribution warehousing, order processing, inventory level of finished goods and customer service.

Due to the above significant contributions, these material management and physical distribution management functions that emerged during this period often resulted into their own pyramid of organisational structures that reported to the various management heads. The objective of this era was to control costs and output was the survival of the firm in the competitive market due to their price-based competitive capability.

Internally Integrated Business Function Era (1980s)

With the beginning of 1980s, business situations became more critical as both external and internal forces continued to generate change in the business functions mainly due to the following reasons:

(*a*) Transportation could no longer be considered to be stable factor in the business planner's equation, as fuel prices continuously soared owing to the OPEC oil embargo followed by deregulation of common carrier transportation;

(*b*) Inflation continued at an unprecedented rate and resulted into significantly higher interest rates;

(*c*) Production productivity was almost at a peak and it was very difficult. to further "cream the fat "in the production function;

(*d*) There was a gradual change in the economic system of most of the countries, especially with regard to multinational operations.

The entire situation had further increased in the quantum of competition in the marketplace. Under above market scenario, firms were continuously experiencing multiplying distribution and operating costs and compelled managers to recapitulate and analyse further reduction in their logistical costs by increased integration of business functions in general and distribution functions in particular. That is why managers were of the opinion that material management, manufacturing management and physical distribution functions should be integrated and the term logistics became the common way to describe the whole activity of storage and movement. This, in the early 1980s, there had been a shift in the positioning of physical distribution and material management functions to an integrated logistics management which combined distribution, manufacturing and materials management functions in order to have a synchronised system which would ensure a smooth flow of all kinds of goods.

Integrated logistics refers to a set of activities concerned with the flow of all materials, information and control system. In an integrated logistics system, there is an interface between traditional activities of physical distribution and material management along with other functions of marketing and manufacturing such as production planning and scheduling, sales forecasting, inventory management, and customer service.

Internal integration of logistics activities became very popular and wide spread in the corporate world during the mid 1980s. So, the National Council of Physical Distribution Management encouraged the trend by changing its name to the council of Logistics Management in 1985.

The major objective behind the development of an integrated logistics management system was cost reduction, which reflects maximisation of profitable sales volume by means of a high degree of coordination between various managerial functions. The output of the era contributed a lot in the overall performance of corporate enterprises in terms of increased productivity, profitability and market share.

Externally Integrated Business Function Era (1990s)

With the beginning of the 1990s, the overall business scenario became more critical, mainly due to the following sea change in the environmental factors:

(*a*) Liberalisation of almost all the economies of the world for the movement of goods from one country to another resulted into world class competition in the market. In such an environment of buyer's market a new pattern for survival emerged by providing the most value for the lowest cost, *i.e.* in terms of best quality product at least costs. Firms started adopting the concept of Total Quality Management (TQM) widely throughout the industry. The idea of zero defects in products and services quickly purvated in the logistical operations in the form of in time and intact delivery.

(*b*) Rapid innovations in the field of science and technology, particularly information technology, have completely changed the corporate mindset from— stock mechanism to real-time response mechanism by means of rapid communication and exchange of data.

(*c*) New inventory management techniques like MRP, DRP and JIT became popular instruments to efficiently plan and deploy inventory items through out the complex and multi-level networks, preventing stock-out situation without enough safety stock, resulting into further curtailment of logistical costs in general and inventory costs in particular. For this particular purpose, firms need to have the most reliable, quality conscious and limited number of suppliers of raw materials and components with the capability to meet requirements at a short notice.

(*d*) Due to increase in the quantum of competition, firms need to have long-term unbeatable core competency or competitive advantage. That is why, it has become the need of the hour for corporate enterprises to keep their immediate customers (marketing intermediaries) happy, loyal and well motivated towards trade by offering their best services as quality, price and promotion.

(*e*) Emergence of third-party logistical service provider changed the entire concept of the transport industry from mere transporters to logistics service solution providers, contributing significantly in the success of logistics system. That is why there has been considerable growth in the third party logistics service industry that provides value-added logistics service to the corporate world and allows them to concentrate on their core competencies in the field of production and marketing.

Hence, due to the above mentioned reasons, the organisations' structure emerge following the logistics activities in the 1990s follows the pattern of external integration, which has given impetus to the concept of Supply Chain Management.

So, the major objective of this era is the core competency by means of further streamlining the logistics system with other supply chain members so as to achieve a higher level of specialisation, and to reduce financial risks. The output of this era is the maximisation of customer value and harmonious long-run relationships between all supply chain members.

In the twenty-first century, logistics should be viewed as a part of management and has four subdivisions:

Business Logistics : That part of the supply chain process that plans, implements, and controls the efficient, effective flow and storage of goods, services, and related information from point of origin to point of use or consumption in order to meet customer requirements.

Military Logistics : *The design and integration of all aspects of support for the operational capability of the military forces (deployed or in garrison) and their equipment to ensure readiness, reliability, and efficiency*

Event Logistics : The network of activities, facilities, and personnel required to organise, schedule, and deploy the resources for an event to take place and to efficiently withdraw after the event.

Service Logistics : The acquisition, scheduling, and management of the facilities, assets, personnel, materials to support and sustain a service operation or business.

All four subdivisions have some common characteristics and requirements such as forecasting, scheduling, and transportation, but they also have some differences in terms of their primary purpose. All four, however, can be viewed in a supply chain context, that is, upstream and down stream there are other organisations that play a role in their overall success and long–run viability

According to Coyle, Bardi and langley general definition that could be used that appears to encompass all four sub disciplines is: Logistics is the process of anticipating customer needs and wants; acquiring the capital, materials, people, technologies, and information necessary to meet those needs and wants; optimising the goods or service-producing network to fulfill customer request; and utilising the network to fulfill customer requests in a timely way.

VALUE–ADDED ROLE OF LOGISTICS

Types of Utility

Four principal types of economic utility add value to a product or service. Included are form, time, place, and possession. Generally, we credit manufacturing activities with providing form utility, logistics activities with time and place utility and marketing activities with possession utility.

What

Form Utility : Form utility refers to the value added to goods through a manufacturing, production, or assembly process. For example, form utility results when raw materials are combined in some predetermined manner to make a finished product. That is the case, for example, when a bottling firm adds together syrup, water and carbonation to make a soft drink. The simple process of adding the raw materials together to produce the soft drink represents a change in product form that adds value to the product. In today's economic environment, certain logistics activities can also provide form utility.[7] For example, breaking bulk and product mixing, which typically take place at distribution centers, change a product's form by changing its shipment size and packaging characteristics. Thus, unpacking a pallet of breakfast cereal into individual consumer-size boxes adds form utility to the product. However, the two principal ways in which logistics adds value are in place and time utility.

Where

Place Utility : Logistics provides place utility by moving goods from production surplus points to points where demand exists. Logistics extends the physical boundaries of the market area, thus adding economic value to the goods. This addition to the economic value of goods or services is known as place utility. Logistics create place utility primarily through transportation. For example, moving farm produce by rail or truck from farm areas to markets where consumers need this produce creates place utility. The same is also true when steel is moved to a plant where the steel is used to make another product. The market boundary extension added by place utility increases competition, which usually leads to lowers prices and increased product availability.

When

Time Utility : Not only must goods and services be available where consumers need them, but they must also be at that point when customers demand them. This is called time utility, or the economic value added to a good or service by having at a demand point at a specific time. Logistics creates time utility through proper inventory maintenance and the strategic location of goods and services. For example, logistics creates time utility by heavily advertised and sale merchandise available in retail stores at precisely the time promised in the advertising copy.

To some extent, transportation may create time utility by moving something more quickly to a point of demand. For example, substituting air transportation for warehousing adds time utility. Time utility is much more important today because of the emphasis upon reducing lead time and minimizing inventory levels through logistics-related strategies such as JIT inventory control.

Why

Possession Utility : Possession utility is a primarily created through the basic marketing activities related to the promotion of products or services. We may define promotion as the effort, through direct and indirect contact with the customer, to increase the desire to possess a good or to benefit from a service. The role of logistics in the economy depends upon the existence of possession utility, for time or place utility make sense only if demand for the product or service exists. It is also true that marketing depends upon logistics, since possession utility cannot be acted upon unless time and place utility services are provided. Order fulfillment is the critical and often first step for meeting customer requirements.

LOGISTICS IN THE FIRM: THE MICRO DIMENSIONS

Another dimension of logistics is the micro perspective, which examines the relationship between logistics and other functional areas in a company—marketing, manufacturing/operations, finances and accounting, and others. Logistics, by its nature, focuses upon processes that cut across traditional functional areas, particularly in today's environment with its emphasis upon the supply chain[8]. Consequently, logistics interfaces in many important ways with all other functional areas.

Logistics Interfaces with Operations /Manufacturing

Length of Production Runs : A classic interface area between logistics and manufacturing management relates to the length of the production run. Production economies are typically associated with long production runs with infrequent production line setups or changeovers. These can, however, easily result in excessive inventories of certain finished products and in limited supplies of others. Thus, the ultimate production decision requires management to carefully weigh the advantages and disadvantages of long versus short production runs. Many industries today tend toward shorter production runs and toward doing whatever it stake to reduce the time and expense normally associated with changing production lines from one product to another. This is particularly true for firms employing the just-in-time (JIT) approach inventory and scheduling. The trend is toward "pull" systems manufacturing/logistics systems where the product is 'pulled' in response to demand as opposed to being "pushed "in advance of demand. The lower inventory levels decrease logistics costs.

Seasonal Demand : The production manager is interested in minimising the effects of seasonal demand for products. Fully anticipating such demand is not always possible, however; thus, having desired product quantities available when and where needed is not always possible. For example, cold weather and snow accumulation in various parts of the country easily influence sales of snow accumulation in various parts of the country easily influence sales of snow skis or snowmobiles. To keep costs low, to avoid overtime and rush situations, and to prepare for the sales schedule, production managers usually like to produce well ahead of the season and to produce a maximum amount. Such advance production may not be economically feasible because of inventory storage costs. However, production managers have to consider this problem in an attempt to keep production costs down. Therefore logistics department, in conjunction with production or manufacturing, must be prepared to accept seasonal inventory, which can start to accumulate three to six months before sales occur.

Supply-side Interfaces : Since the logistics manager is responsible for the inbound movement and storage of raw materials that will feed the production line, logistics and production also interface on the supply side. A shortage or stock out situation could result in the shut down of a production facility or an increase in production costs. The logistics manager should ensure that available quantities of raw materials and other production inputs are sufficient to meet production schedules yet are conservative in terms of inventory carrying costs. Because of the need for this type of coordination, many firms today have shifted the responsibility for production scheduling from manufacturing to logistics management. The end result is a broadening of overall logistics responsibility.

Protective Packaging : Another activity at the interface of logistics and operations is packaging, which many firms treat as a logistics activity. In the context of either operations or logistics management, the principal purpose that that packaging serves to protect the product from damage. This is distinct from whatever value the package may for marketing or promotional reasons.

Foreign and Third Party Alternatives : The interface between logistics operations is becoming more critical, given recent interest in the procurement of raw materials and other production inputs from foreign sources. Also, many firms today are making arrangements with third-party manufacturers, or 'co-packers', to produce or assemble some or all of the firms' finished products. These arrangements are especially prevalent in the food industry, where many firms manufacture only food items to be sold under someone else's label.

Logistics Interfaces with Marketing : *Marketing Mix:* Logistics is sometimes referred to as the other half of marketing. The rationale for this definition is that the physical distribution or outbound side of a firm's logistics system is responsible for the physical movement and storage of goods for customers and thus plays an important role in selling a product. In some instances, physical distribution and order fulfillment may be the key variables in selling a product; that is your ability to provide the product at the right time in the right quantities may be the critical element in making a sale.

There is interface between logistics and marketing activities in each principal area of the marketing mix. The material is organised according to the four *Ps* of marketing—Price, Product, Promotion, and Place.

Price : From a logistics perspective, adjusting quantity prices to conform with shipment sizes appropriate for transportation companies may be quite important. Rail roads, for example, publish minimum weight requirements for carload lots—for instance, 30,000 kgs. Motor carriers typically publish minimum four or five rates that will apply to the same commodity shipped between two points depending upon size (weight) of the shipment. The larger the size, the lower the unit rate charged. In other words, a price discount schedule for shipping larger volumes at one time applies because the transportation company experiences economy if the customer sends larger shipments.

Matching Schedules : Companies selling products also typically provide a discount schedule for larger purchase quantities. If such discount schedules relate to transportation rate discount schedules in terms of weight, the company may able to save itself some money or save money for customers, depending on the sale terms. For example, if a company sells on a delivered–price basis (price includes transportation charges) and if its price schedule matches the transportation shipping requirements on a weight basis, the company should be able to get lower rates with larger purchases and thus save money. So when the company calculates the number of units that it wants to sell to a customer for a particular price, it should see how the weight of that number of units compares with the weight requirements for a transportation rate. In many instances, increasing the quantity purchased in order to produce a total shipment weight that will qualify for a lower per unit transportation weight becomes advantageous. Even if the firm were selling goods on a free on board (FOB) point-of-origin basis (transportation charges paid by the buyer), this approach would enable the firm's customers to qualify for the lower rate and thus save money.

Although, it is not always possible to adjust prices to meet rate breaks and to have a quantity to deal with, organisation should investigate such alternatives. In some organisations, entire pricing schedules conform to various quantities the company can ship by motor and rail road or by other modes of transportation. Under legislation in USA *i.e.* Robinson-Pitman Act and related legislation, transportation cost savings are a valid reason for offering a price discount.

Volume Relationships : In addition logistics manager may be interested in the volume sold under different price schedules because this will affect inventory requirements, replacement times and other aspects of customer service. Although this is somewhat difficult to analyse, affirm may consider the logistics ability to provide sufficient volumes within an attractive price schedule. Such a situation may be particularly true when price specials generate extra sales at particular times of the year.

Product : Another decision frequently made in the marketing area concerns products, particularly their physical attributes. Their size, shape, weight, packaging, and other physical dimensions affect the ability of the logistics system to move and store products. Therefore, logistics manager should offer input when marketing is deciding upon the physical dimensions of new products. The logistics manager can supply appropriate information about the movement and storage of the new products.

In addition to new products, firms frequently refurbish old products in one way or another to improve and maintain sales. The physical dimensions of products affect the use of storage and movement systems. They affect the carriers that a firm can use, equipment needed, damage rates, storage ability, use of materials–handling equipment such as conveyors and pallets, exterior packaging, and many other logistics aspects.

It is very difficult to convey the frustration that some logistics managers experience when discovering a change in the product package that makes the use of standard size pallets uneconomical, or that uses trailer or boxcar space inefficiently or in a way that could damage products for example, when Gillette first introduced the Daisy Razor, the logistics group did not learn until late in the game that they had to deal with light and bulky floor stand displays, with consequent low weight density. Not only would the floor stand displays not fit on the warehouse conveyors but they to be shipped at a rate that was 150 per cent higher than the existing rate for the product itself. Gillette eventually corrected the situation but it was an expensive lesson.

Consumer Packaging

Another marketing area that affects logistics is consumer packaging. The marketing manager often regards consumer packaging as a “silent” salesperson. At the retail level, the package may be a determining factor in influencing sales. The marketing manager will be concerned about package appearance, information provided, and other related aspects; for a customer comparing several products on the retailer’s shelf, the consumer package may make the sale. The consumer package is important to the logistics manager for several reasons. The consumer packages usually have to fit into what is called the industrial package, or the external package. The size, shape and other dimensions of the consumer package will affect the use of the industrial packages. The protection the consumer offers also concerns the logistics manager.

The physical dimensions and the protection aspects of consumer packages affect the logistics system in the areas of transportation, material handling, and warehousing.

Promotion

Promotion is a marketing area that receives much attention in an organisation. Firms often spend hundreds of thousands or even millions of rupees on national advertising campaign and other promotional activities to improve a sales position.

An organisation making a promotional effort to stimulate sales should inform its logistics manager so that sufficient in inventory quantities will be available for distribution to the customer. But even when logistics is informed, problems can occur. For example, when Gillette introduced the disposable twin-blade Good News razor, the company's original plan called for three consecutive promotions. The national launch promotion was to achieve sales of twenty million units. A following trade deal promotion was to net ten million in sales, and Gillette expected a third promotional campaign to net an additional twenty million—for a total of fifty in sales. As it turned, the first promotion sold thirty five million—seventy-five percent over the plan. Needless to say, this quite a burden on the logistics group to try to meet the demand.

Push *versus* Pull

We should look beyond the simple relationship between increasing and analysing basic promotion strategies to see how they affect the logistics department. Marketing managers often classify their promotion strategies into two basic categories: push or pull. What they are implying is that they can try to either 'pushing' the product through the distribution channel to the customer or 'pulling' it through.

Channel Competition

Producers frequently compete to get distribution channels to give their products the sales effort they feel their products deserve. For example, a cereal producer may want to ensure sufficient space for its product on the retailer's shelf or ensure that wholesalers hold product quantities sufficient to satisfy retailers, believing that ultimately the final consumer demand for the product will influence the retailer and the wholesaler. By selling popular products, they improve their profitability. The higher the product turnover, the more likely they are to make a profit; the happier they are with a particular product, the more willing they are to give it space and a better position in the store.

Pull Strategy

Companies can attempt to improve their sales by *pulling* their product through distribution channel with national advertising. Promotional advertising attempts to create or stimulate sales to customers into the retail store asking for a product they have seen advertised in a magazine, have heard advertised on the radio, or more likely, have seen advertised on television. The purchase will likely influence the retailer, and the retailer will influence the wholesaler, if any, from whom the retailer purchases. Some companies feel that the best approach in promoting a product is to pull it through distribution channels by directly stimulating demand at the consumer level.

Push Strategy

The other basic approach is the push method. Implied in the push approach is cooperation with the channels of distribution to stimulate customer sales-in other words, producers may pay part of local advertising costs or provide special store displays to stimulate sales. In cooperating with the wholesaler, a manufacturer may be able to offer retailers a special price at a particular time to stimulate product demand. The emphasis is upon having the distribution channel work with the company. This contrasts with the pull approach, wherein the company stimulates sales somewhat independently of the retailer by national advertising or by advertising a product on a broad regional scale.

Logistics Impact

In fact, some companies combine the two in their promotion efforts. From the logistics manager's point of view, however push and pull are often different as far as logistics system requirements are concerned. The pull approach is more likely to generate erratic demand that is difficult to predict and that may place emergency demands upon the logistics system. Broad-scale national advertising has the potential to be extremely successful, but predicting consumer response to new products is often difficult. Such advertising may also strain the logistics system, requiring emergency shipments and higher transportation. Frequent stock outs may also result, requiring additional inventory. The Gillette situation is an example of such a case. On the other hand, a push approach may have a more orderly demand pattern. Cooperation with the retailer allows manufacturers to fill the 'pipeline' somewhat in advance of the stimulated sales rather than quickly, on an almost emergency basis, as retailers and consumers clamour for some successfully promoted new product.

PLACE: Wholesalers Vs. Retailers

The place decision refers to the distribution channels and thus involves both transactional and physical distribution. Marketers typically become more involved in making decisions about marketing transactions and in deciding such things as whether to sell a product to wholesalers or to deal directly with the retailers. From the logistics manager's point of view, such decisions may significantly affect logistics system requirement. For example, companies dealing only with wholesalers will probably have fewer logistics problems than will companies dealing directly with retailers. From the logistics manager's point of view, such decision may significantly affect logistics system requirements. For example, companies dealing only with wholesalers will probably have fewer logistics problems than will the companies dealing directly with retailers. Wholesalers, on the average, tend to purchase in larger quantities than do retailers and to place their orders and manage their inventories more predictably and consistently, thereby making the logistics manager's job easier. Retailing establishment, particularly small retailers, often order in small quantities and do not always allow sufficient lead time for replenishment before stock outs. Consequently manufacturers may need to purchase time-sensitive transportation service at a premium price to meet delivery needs.

Recent Trends: Customer Service

Perhaps the most significant trend is that marketers have begun to recognise the strategic value of place in the marketing mix and the increased revenues and customer satisfaction that may result from high-quality logistical services. As a result, many firms have recognised customer service as the interface activity between marketing and logistics and have aggressively and effectively promoted customer service as a key element of the marketing mix. Firms in industries such as food, chemicals and pharmaceuticals have reported considerable success along these lines.

LOGISTICS INTERFACES WITH OTHER FACES

While manufacturing and marketing are probably the two most important internal, functional interfaces for logistics in a product company, there are other important interfaces. The finance area has become increasingly important during the last decade. The impact that logistics can have upon return on assets (ROA) or return on investment (ROI) is very significant.

ROA = revenue-expenses/assets

Or

ROA = gross profit/assets

Logistics can impact ROA positively in several ways. Inventory is an asset on the balance sheet; lowering inventory (assets) in the preceding equation increases ROA. In addition to inventory, there has been improvement to the utilization of other logistics related assets, namely, warehouse and transportation equipment investment. It is also pointed out earlier that logistics cost have been reduced in some companies, which improves gross margin or gross profit and increases ROA. Finally, the focus upon customer service can increase revenue or sales. As long as the increase in sales is not offset by higher cost by higher cost for customer service, then ROA will also be increased.[9]

Accounting is also an important interface for logistics. Accounting systems are critical for providing appropriate cost information for analysis of alternative logistics systems. Far too often in the past, logistics-related cost were not measured specifically and were often lumped into overhead, which made it extremely difficult to systematically monitor logistics cost. The recent interest in direct product profitability and the related cost accounting systems such as activity-based costing (ABC) has been beneficial to improving the quality of logistics analyses. Accounting systems are also critical for measuring supply chain trade-offs and performance.

LOGISTICAL FUNCTIONS

The various definitions discussed earlier indicate activities for which logistics manager may be responsible. These are:

- Traffic and transportation
- Warehousing and storage
- Industrial packaging
- Materials handling
- Inventory control
- Order fulfillment
- Demand forecasting
- Production planning
- Purchasing
- Customer service levels
- Plant and warehouse site selection
- Return goods handling
- Parts and service support
- Salvage and scrap disposal

This list is quite comprehensive. Some companies with well-organised logistics areas may not place responsibility for all of these activities within the logistics area. For example, companies having a physical distribution focus may not include procurement in their logistics organisation.

Scope of Activities

The development of interest in logistics after World War II contributed to the growth in activities associated with the logistics. Given the scope of this growth, it is worthwhile to discuss these activities and their relationship to logistics.

Transportation

Transportation is a very important part of the logistics system. A major focus in logistics is upon the physical movement or flow of goods or upon the network that moves that moves the product. This network is composed of transportation agencies that provide the service for the firm. The logistics manager is responsible for selecting the mode or modes of transportation used in moving the raw materials and finished goods or for developing private transportation as an alternative.

Storage

Transportation Trade Off : A second area, which has a trade-off relationship with transportation, is storage. It involves two separate but closely related activities: inventory management and warehousing. a direct relationship exists between transportation and the level of inventory and number of warehouses required. For example, if firms use a relatively slow means of transport, they usually have to keep higher inventory level and usually have more warehousing space for this inventory. They may examine the possibility of using faster transport to eliminate some of these warehouses and inventory stored therein.

Materials Handling : A fourth area to be considered is materials handling, which is also of interest to other areas in the typical manufacturing organisation. Materials handling is important to efficient warehouse operation. Logistics managers are concerned with the movement of goods into a warehouse, the placement of goods in a warehouse, and the movement of goods from storage to order-picking areas and eventually to dock areas for transportation out of the warehouse. Materials handling is usually concerned with mechanical equipment for short-distance movement; such equipment includes conveyors, forklift trucks, overhead cranes, and containers. Production managers may want a particular pallet or container or container type that is not compatible with logistics warehousing activities. Therefore, the materials-handling designs must be coordinated in order to ensure congruity between the types of equipment used. In addition, the company may find it economical to use the same type of forklift trucks in the plants and in the warehouses.

Order Fulfillment

Another activity area that logistics may control is order fulfillment, which generally consists of activities involved with completing customer orders. Initially, one might question why the logistics area would concern itself directly with order fulfillment. However, one important physical distribution factor is the time elapsing from the time when a customer decides to place an order for a product until the time that those goods are actually delivered in a satisfactory condition, that is, the lead time.

For example, assume that the present system takes a total. lead time of eight days for transmittal, processing, order preparation, and shipping. Order processing may take four days, and order preparation may take an additional two days, which means that the goods have to be transported to the customer in two days. The short delivery time may require a premium means of transportation. If order processing is considered part of the logistics system, then the company might examine improvements, such as using telephone calls and more computer equipment for processing to reduce order processing time to two days or less. This would allow the firm to use much cheaper transportation and still get the goods to the customer within eight days. Looking from a time perspective or in terms of total lead time we can see that order fulfillment is quite important to the logistics function.

Inventory Accuracy

Forecasting : Another activity important to the logistics area is inventory forecasting. Accurate forecasting of inventory requirements an materials and parts is essential to effective inventory control. This is particularly true in companies using a just-in-time (JIT) or materials requirement planning (MRP) approach to control inventory. Logistics personnel should develop forecasts in those situations to ensure accuracy and effective control. Too frequently, forecasts developed by marketing staff reflect sales objectives rather than inventory requirements.

Production Planning : Another area of growing interest for logistics managers is production planning, which is closely related to forecasting in terms of effective inventory control. Once a forecast is developed and the current inventory on the hand and usage rate is assessed, production managers can determine the number of units necessary to ensure adequate market coverage. However, in multiple-product firms, production process timing and certain product line relationships require close coordination with logistics or actual control of production planning by logistics. The integration of production planning into logistics is becoming increasingly common in large corporations.

Purchasing : Purchasing, or procurement, is another activity that we can include in logistics. The basic rationale for including purchasing in logistics is that transportation cost relates directly to the geographic location (distance) of raw materials and component parts purchased for a company's production needs. In terms of transportation and inventory costs, the quantities purchased would also affect logistics cost. Including purchasing within the logistics area is primarily a matter of whether this more effectively coordinates and lowers costs for the firm. As was noted previously, a growing number of companies added purchasing to the logistics function during the 1970s and 1980s.

Customer Service : Another area of importance is customer service. Customer service is a complex topic and one that concerns other functional company areas. Customer service levels in many ways glue together other logistics areas. Decisions about inventory, transportation, and warehousing relate to customer service requirements. While areas. Customer service levels in many ways glue together other logistics areas. Decisions about inventory, transportation, and warehousing relate to customer service requirements. While customarily the logistics area does not completely control customer service decisions, logistics plays an extremely important role in ensuring that the customer gets the right product at the right place and time. Logistics decisions about product availability and inventory lead time are critical to customer service.

Site Location : Another area is important to logistics is plant and warehouse site location. We discuss this activity at some length in a later chapter. A location change could alter time and place relationships between plants and markets or between supply points and plants. Such changes will affect transportation rates and service, customer service, inventory requirements, and possibly other areas. Therefore, the logistics manager is quite concerned about location decisions. In fact, plant location, as discussed in a subsequent chapter, is frequently as important as warehouse location. Transportation cost is frequently as important as warehouse location. Transportation cost is frequently a very important factor in deciding on a location.

Other Activities : Other areas may be considered a part of logistics. Areas such as parts and service support, return goods handling, and salvage and scrape disposal indicate the reality of logistical activities managed in companies producing consumer durables or industrial products. Here, a very integrative approach is necessary. Logistics offers input into product design as well as into maintenance and supply services, since transportation and storage decisions affect these areas. (The definitions of logistics and materials management imply the importance of such activities to systematic logistics management in such companies.)

APPROACHES TO ANALYSING LOGISTICS SYSTEMS

The analysis of logistics systems frequently requires different views or perspectives of logistical activities. The best perspective to take depends upon the type of analysis that is needed. For example, if a company wants to analyse the long-run system design of its logistics system, a view of logistics that focuses upon the company's network of node and link relationships would probably be most beneficial[10]. On the other hand, if a company is evaluating a change in a carrier or mode of transportation, it should probably analyse the logistics system in terms of cost centers. In this section, we discuss four approaches for analyzing logistics systems: Materials management *vs.* physical distribution, cost centers, nodes *vs.* links, and logistics channels.

Materials Management Vs. Physical Distribution

The Classification of logistics into materials management and physical distribution (inbound and outbound logistics) is very useful to logistics management or control in an organisation. Frequently, the movement and storage of raw materials in a firm is different from the movement and storage of finished products. For example, a steel company may move required raw materials of iron ore and coal by barge and large rail carload. Storage may require nothing more elaborate than land where these items can be dumped and piled for future use. On the other hand, the finished steel will very often be moved by motor carrier, and storage will require an enclosed facility for protection against the elements and, perhaps, elaborate materials-handling equipment.

Cost Differences

The different logistics requirement that may exist between materials management and physical distribution may have important implications for the design of an organisation's logistics system. Great differences may result in different logistics system designs for materials management and physical distribution. Companies may find it convenient to view their logistics system from these two perspectives, and somewhat different management approaches for each may result. In spite of such differences, close coordination between materials management and physical distribution is still necessary. Additional perspectives related to viewing logistics in terms of materials management/in-bound logistics and physical distribution/out-bound logistics deserve consideration. In fact, from the inbound and outbound requirements perspective, we may classify companies into four different types of logistics systems.

Balanced System

Some companies have a reasonably balanced flow heavy inbound flow on the inbound and outbound sides of their logistics system. In other words, they receive supplies from various vendors in different locations and ship to various customers in different locations. Consumer product companies such as General Foods, Pillsbury and General Mills typically fit this description. While these companies may emphasise the physical distribution or out-bound side because of the importance of customer service, both in-bound and out-bound logistics are important.

Heavy In-bound

Some companies have a very heavy in-bound flow and very simple out-bound flow. An aircraft such as Boeing is a good example. It uses thousands of parts manufactured by hundreds of vendors to assemble and produce a finished airplane. Once the air plane is finished and tested, the company simply flies it to the customer (Delta Airlines, for example), who ordered it two or three years before delivery. The process requires no warehousing, special transportation arrangements, or packaging. In contrast, the inbound side requires detailed scheduling, coordination, and planning to ensure that parts arrive in time. Varying lead times for parts from vendors present a complex logistics challenge. Auto manufacturing, using twelve thousand to thirteen thousand parts per car, also fit this model. Their outbound systems, while more complex than Aircraft Company's is not nearly as complex as their outbound systems.

Heavy Out-bound

A chemical company like Dow offers a good example of a logistics system with heavy outbound flow. In-bound crude oil by-products, salt water, and other raw materials flow from a limited number of sources and frequently move in volume over relatively short distances. On the out-bound side, a wide variety of industrial and consumer products are produced that need storage, packaging, and transportation to the final customer. Therefore, in a company with heavy out-bound, the physical distribution side of logistics system is more complex.

Reverse Systems

Some companies have reverse flows on the out-bound side of their logistics systems. This is true of companies producing durable products that the customer may return for trade-in, for repairs, or for salvage and disposal. Companies that produce computers, telephone equipment, and copy machines have these characteristics. Companies that deal with returnable containers also fit this model. Increased concern with the environment will require more companies to develop reverse logistics systems to dispose of packaging materials on used products.

Cost Centres

It is previously mentioned that the management activities that many firms include in the logistics area, namely transportation, warehousing, inventory, materials handling and industrial packaging. It is also emphasised the need to consider these activities as being highly interrelated. By looking at these activities as cost centres, one can analyse possible trade-offs between and among them that could result in lower overall cost and/or better service.

Trade-offs

The breakdown of logistics into various cost centers or activity centers represents a second approach to logistics system analysis. Firms frequently analyse logistics systems by dividing them into cost or activity centers, since reducing total logistics costs and/or improving service most frequently occurs by trading off one activity centre against another. For example, shifting from rail to motor carrier may result, because of faster and more reliable service, in lower inventory costs, which offsets the higher motor carrier rate. The activity or cost centre perspective is very useful in reviewing various trades-offs for lower cost and/or improved service to the customer or plants.

Nodes *Vs.* Links

A third approach to analszing the logistics system in an organisation is in terms of nodes and links. The nodes are established spatial points where goods stop for storage or processing. In other words, the nodes are plants and warehouses where the organisation stores materials for conversion into finished products or goods in finished form for sale to customers (equalisation of supply and demand).

The other part of the system is the links, which represent the transportation network connecting the nodes in the logistics system. The network can be composed of individual modes of transportation (rail, motor, air, water, or pipelines) and of combination and variations. From a node-link perspective, the complexity of logistics systems can vary enormously. One-node systems may use a simple link from suppliers to a combined plant and warehouse and then to customers in a relatively small market area. At the other end of the spectrum are large, multi product firms with multiple plant and warehouse locations. The complex transportation networks of the latter may include three or four different modes and perhaps private as well as for- hire transportation.

The node and link perspective, in allowing analysis of a logistics system's two basic elements, represent a convenient basis for seeking possible system improvements. As it is noted, the complexity of a logistics system often relates directly to the various time and distance relationships between nodes and the links and to the regularity, predictability, and volume of flow of goods entering, leaving, and moving within the system.

Logistics Channel

A fourth approach to logistics system analysis is to study the logistics channel, the network of intermediaries engaged in transfer, storage, handling, communication, and other functions that contribute to the efficient flow of goods. We can view the logistics channel as part of the total distribution channel, which includes, in addition to the logistical flow, a transaction flow of specific interest to the marketing specialist. The logistical channel can be simple or complex. In simple channel an individual producer deals directly with a final customer. The control in this channel is relatively simple. The individual manufacturer controls the logistical flows since it with the customer. Another channel is multi-echelon channel which is more complex, consist a market warehouse and retailers. The market warehouse could be a public warehouse. In this instance, the control is more difficult because of the additional storage and transportation.

The other channel is complex, comprehensive channel. In this channel, the task of achieving an effective logistical flow in the channel is far more formidable. This channel portrays the situation confronting many large organisations.

Some instances involving production of a basic good like steel, aluminum, or chemicals may further complicate the situation because companies may be a part of more than one channel. For example, the steel may be sold to auto manufacturers, container manufacturers, or the file cabinet producers. Duplication of storage facilities, small shipment transportation, conflict over mode choices, and other problems may contribute to inefficiency in the channel. Communication problem may exist.

REFERENCES

1. Logistics : The Next Big Growth Driver Article by V. Shunmugum and Ritambhara Singh *Business Line*, Saturday, March 29, 2008, p. 8.
2. *Logistical Management—The Integrated Supply Chain Process* by Donald J. Bowersox, David J. Closs –Tata McGra-Hill, 2nd Edition New Delhi, 2006, p. 56-86.
3. www. wikipaedia–the concept of logistics.
4. *The Management of Business Logistics—A Supply Chain Perspective* by Coyle, Bardi, Langley, Thompson Press, 2nd Edition New Delhi, 2006, p. 36-52.
5. *Logistical Management—The Integrated Supply Chain Process* by Donald J. Bowersox, David J. Closs, Tata McGraw Hill, 2nd Edition, New Delhi, 2006, p. 45-49.
6. *Containerisation and Multimodal Transport in India* by Dr. KV Hariharan, Shroff Publication, New Delhi, 2007, p. 20-34.
7. *The Management of Business Logistics—A Supply Chain Perspective* by Coyle, Bardi, Langley-Thompson Press 2nd Edition, New Delhi, 2006, p. 56-64.
8. *Logistics Management* by Reji Ismail-Excel Books, New Delhi, 1st Edition, 2007, p. 23-28.
9. *Logistical Management—The Integrated Supply Chain Process* by Donald J. Bowersox, David J. Closs –Tata McGraw –Hill, 2nd Edition, New Delhi, 2006, p. 92-101.
10. *Logistics Management –Indian* Edition by Reed Infomedia India, Vol. 1, issue 1, April 2007.

Logistics Management Practices in India

Chapter 2

Logistics as a sector might not be the most glamorous one but it is certainly one of those sectors in India which is poised for a period of high sustained growth. The huge investments that is happening across sectors like retail where supply chain management is the key to success and the tremendous growth that is exhibited in foreign trade will act as big power boosters for this sector. Coupled with this the progressive liberalisation that is happening in logistics and massive capital expenditure plans in various sectors of economy will aid the positive sentiments associated with the sector. For example, the Planning Commission of India has estimated that the total infrastructure spend of India in the 11th plan would be nearly $500 bn and our Government has also reformed customs and excise procedures and made the environment more friendly for logistics companies by introducing tonnage tax and value added tax.[1]

SECTOR SNAPSHOT

The total size of the logistics sector in India at the end of 2007 (*Source:* CII Report on Logistics) is $90 bn. Total logistics related costs as a per cent of the GDP is estimated at about 13 per cent in India where as it is just 11 per cent in

Japan, 10 per cent in Europe and 9 per cent in US. The high cost structure in India is due to the inefficiencies at various points of the chain and also due to the regulatory bottle necks.[2] This in a way reflects the need for enormous investment that this sector has to make for improving its productivity and the logistics sector of India seems to be doing exactly the same. Automotive, IT hardware and FMCG have emerged as the major users of Third Party Logistics services. The consistent 8 per cent p. a. growth rate that India is likely to witness in the near future will help the logistics sector to reach a size of $125 bn in 2010 and $180 bn in 2012. Road transport is the biggest segment in the logistics sector and it accounts for nearly 70 per cent of the total logistics sector. The aggregate length of roads in India is at about 3. 34 mn kilometer. Assuming a growth rate of 9.9 per cent the expected road freight volume is 1231 billion kilometer by the year 2012.[3] An estimated 1.2 mn trucks crisscross the roads of the country. The sector is characterised by high level of competition and low net profit margin. Cost is the main differentiation factor in this segment since users are more cost sensitive than time sensitive. Road transportation in the country is similar to retail sector in a way since it is highly unorganised with majority of the truck owners having less than five trucks. One of the fastest growing segments inside logistics is the express services industry and globally itself this industry is growing at about two and half times the world GDP growth rate.

MAJOR SEGMENTS IN THE LOGISTICS SECTOR

Logistics sector that has grown at a fast pace in India and the main volume contributors are petroleum, liquefied gas, chemicals and vegetable oil. This is a segment which is asset intensive as well as one which requires a lot of technical expertise. The petrochemical industry growth rate which averaged three to four per cent during the last five years is expected to jump to 12-15 per cent over the next few years. At current prices, the downstream petrochemical industry production is expected to increase from the existing $15-$18 billion to $30-35 billion.[4] Any talk about the logistics sector would not be complete without a mention of the vital role that our ports play in the Indian economy. Over 95 per cent of the total trade in India is sea borne and the total cargo handled at the Indian ports is estimated at 450 million tonnes. By the year 2011-12 this is expected to double to nearly 900 million tonnes. So the growth that is expected in this sector is huge and this is testified by the tremendous increase in India's foreign trade. India's exports in 2007-08 were $155 bn and the target set for the next financial year is $200 bn. Our imports in 2007-08 were $245 bn and this takes the total merchandise trade to $400 bn which is about 40 per cent of the GDP. But even with this level of engagement India's share in the world merchandise trade is just 1.5%, so it can be safely said that we have just scratched the surface and more remains to done to boost our share. This increase in share will certainly translate to good times for logistics sector. The cargo that is transported through ships can be categorized into the following different types like wet cargo, break bulk cargo, dry bulk cargo and containerised cargo. Among these, containerised cargo is the one which is witnessing the highest growth rate. In the fiscal 2008 container traffic at twelve government owned ports rose from 19.03 per cent to 6.6 mn TEU from 5.44 mn TEU.[5]

TEU (TWENTY EQUIVALENT UNITS)

A TEU is standard unit of measurement for a container and it is the abbreviation for twenty foot equivalent unit. It must be remembered that the total container traffic in 1990-91 was just 0.68 mn TEU. The total container business in India is just 30 per cent of the value of India's total external trade and this pales in comparison the global average of 70-75 per cent. At the projected growth rate of 19 per cent India's container traffic will reach a total size of 21 mn TEU by the year 2016 and even this is very small when compared to China's current capacity of 100 mn TEU.[6] The growth in container trans-port business will benefit significantly those involved in the business of running container train operations, multi-modal transport operation (MTO) and ICD/CFS. MTO's arrange the transportation of goods from door to door and they assume contractual obligation for the transportation. Big companies these days are more interested in dealing with MTOs as they provide a single point of contact for all the services. Here goods are transported in different modes and often transported in containers so it can be said that containeri-zation has lead to the growth of these services. Multi modal transport operation is a chain that links different modes like land, sea and air into one single process and this ensures that significant savings in both cost and time. This is a kind of service which provides holistic solutions that covers almost all needs of the users. The advent of containerisation has transformed the concept of cargo delivery system to multi-modal transport operation that has enabled the shift from "port-to-port" to "door-to-door". Supply chain management has emerged as a source of strategic benefit that brings competitive advantage to the firm. According to CARE report, express service industry in our country has grown at the rate of about 33 per cent per annum for the past decade and its size is now estimated to be nearly Rs. 9400 crores.[7] In this industry customers are time sensitive and they demand efficient services. Cost is not a big issue with such customers as they judge the quality of the service providers by using the key parameters like speed of distribution, geographic coverage offered, security and reliability, value added service and customer care. To meet these quality objectives the express industry needs to deploy information technology which in fact is the back bone of the industry. IT helps in the precise monitoring of cargo at every stage of its journey. Multi-modal services help in providing turnkey solutions to clients.

INVESTMENT RATIONALE

Company is an asset intensive business that requires significant technical skills. This will act as an entry barrier to other players. Presence in the auto gas segment that is fast growing because of it being economical as well environment friendly. Has an organic as well as inorganic growth strategy Investment rationale Express logistics is the fast growing segment in the logistics space. Good geographic spread that cannot be easily replicated by other players and support from MNC parent. Great brand equity Investment rationale CONCOR has leadership position in the container rail segment with a market share of 90 per cent. The new private players have not been able to make any impact. Huge capital expenditure plans. It has 58 rail linked terminals and 8300 wagons and it will take private players years to build this kind of infrastructure. Growth in foreign trade and shifting trend towards containerisation of traffic will help the company significantly.[8]

The Indian economy has been growing at an average rate of more than 8 per cent over the last four years putting enormous demands on its productive infrastructure. Whether it is the physical infrastructure of road, ports, water, power etc. or the digital infrastructure of broadband networks, telecommunication etc. or the service infrastructure of logistics—all are being stretched to perform beyond their capabilities. Interestingly, this is leading to an emergence of innovative practices to allow business and public service to operate at a higher growth rate in an environment where the support systems are getting augmented concurrently.

Broadly speaking, the Indian logistics sector, as elsewhere, comprises the entire inbound and outbound segments of the manufacturing and service supply chains. Of late, the logistics infrastructure has received lot of attention both from business and industry as well as policy makers. However, the role of managing this infrastructure (or the logistics management regimen) to effectively compete has been slightly under-emphasised. Inadequate logistics infrastructure has an effect of creating bottlenecks in the growth of an economy; the logistics management regimen has the capability of overcoming the disadvantages of the infrastructure in the short run while providing cutting edge competitiveness in the long term. It is here that exist several challenges as well as opportunities for the Indian economy. There are several models that seem to be emerging based on the critical needs of the Indian economy that can stand as viable models for other global economies as well.

Two key areas that require attention in managing the logistics chains across the Indian business sectors—cost and reliable value add services. Logistics costs (*i.e.*, inventory holding, transportation, warehousing, packaging, losses and related administration costs) have been estimated at 13-14 per cent of Indian GDP which is higher than the 8 per cent of USA's and lower than the 21 per cent of China's GDP. Service reliability of the logistics industry in emerging markets, like India, has been referred to as slow and requiring high engagement time of the customers, thereby, incurring high indirect variable costs. However, the Indian logistics story is one with islands of excellence though there has been a general improvement on almost all parameters.

Some Peculiarities of the Indian Supply Chains

The Indian logistics sector has typically been driven by the objective of reducing transportation costs that were (and often continue to be) inordinately high due to regional concentration of manufacturing and geographically diversified distribution activities as well as inefficiencies in infrastructure and accompanying technology. Freight movement has slowly been shifting from rail to road with implications on quality of transfer, timeliness of delivery and consequently costs except for commodities which over long distances, predominantly, move through the extensive rail network. More on the infrastructure issues later. The transportation industry is fragmented and largely un-organised—a large number of independent players with regional or national permits that carry freight, often with small fleet size of one or two single-axle trucks. This segment carries a large per cent of the national load and almost all of the regional load. This fragmented segment comprises owners and employees with inadequate skills, perspectives or abilities to organize or manage their operations effectively. Low cost has been traditionally achieved by employing low level of technology, low wages (due to lower education levels), poor maintenance of equipment, overloading of the truck beyond capacity, and price competition amongst a large number of service providers in the industry. Often, one finds transportation cartels that regulate supply of trucks and transport costs. However, the long run average cost of transport operations across the entire supply chain may not turn out to be low.

Table 2.1 gives a break up of the logistics cost across different sectors of the Indian industry and the changes therein over the last five years. It shows how the logistics spend is increasing, sometimes dramatically, across various industrial sectors. Steel, pharmaceuticals, food and agro-business, and auto have also been the sectors that are growing most rapidly in the national economy—it is no surprise that their logistics costs have been increasing at a faster rate. A few observations are in order here. The low change in order processing and administrative costs in the cement sector could possibly be due to the use of call centers by various producers for order processing and dispatch planning. Steel and pharmaceutical sectors have seen maximum changes in component costs. The distribution practice of pushing goods down the channel might be responsible for high increase in the inventory and warehousing costs in the pharmaceutical industry. Investments in new cold chains and losses might be the causes of high change in the warehousing, packaging and losses related costs.

Warehousing has also been typically dominated by small players with small capacities and poor deployment of handling, stacking and monitoring technologies. While it has had detrimental effect on almost all sectors, the food sector has been the one that has suffered the most due to low investment in cold chains and allied machinery. Erratic power outages have also meant low dependence on technology and a more manual operation. Another fact that has affected both the location as well cost of operating warehouse has been the "octroi taxi." Firms have been locating warehouses outside city limits.

Table 2.1. Distribution of logistics costs across some sectors (2000-2006)

Sector	Logistics Cost Components (in US $ mn)	Trans-portation	Inven-tory holding	Ware-housing, packaging & loses	Order processing & administrative	Total Logistics cost
Auto	2000-01	285.0	171.0	185.3	71.3	712.6
	2005-06	406.5	243.9	264.3	101.6	1016.4
	Avg.Change	20.3	12.2	13.2	5.1	50.6
Cement	2000-01	50.6	30.4	32.9	12.7	126.5
	2005-06	55.4	33.3	36.0	13.8	138.5
	Avg.Change	4.8	2.9	3.1	1.2	12.0
Consumer Durables	2000-01	331.9	199.1	215.7	83.0	829.6
	2005-06	398.9	239.3	259.3	99.7	997.3
	Avg.Change	11.2	6.7	7.3	2.8	27.9
FMCG	2000-01	201.5	120.9	131.0	50.4	503.8
	2005-06	280.7	168.4	182.5	70.2	701.8
	Avg.Change	13.2	7.9	8.6	3.3	33.0
Food	2000-01	398.7	239.3	259.2	99.7	996.8
	2005-06	524.5	314.7	340.9	131.1	1311.2
	Avg.Change	21.0	12.6	13.6	5.2	52.4
Garment	2000-01	337.3	202.4	219.2	84.3	843.2
	2005-06	454.4	272.6	295.3	113.6	1135.9
	Avg.Change	19.5	11.7	12.7	4.9	48.8
Pharma-ceutical	2000-01	174.0	104.4	113.1	43.5	434.9
	2005-06	310.0	186.0	201.5	77.5	775.0
	Avg.Change	22.7	13.6	14.7	5.7	56.7
Steel	2000-01	438.3	263.0	284.9	109.6	1095.7
	2005-06	693.6	416.1	450.8	173.4	1734.0
	Avg.Change	42.5	25.5	27.7	10.6	106.4

They delay moving goods into retail network as late as possible. It has also led to the development of a unholy business-government nexus to avoid the tax and extract rents. Use of technology is quite limited—both IT and engineering equipments in order to increase productivity and service. An in-appropriate evaluation of the diverse benefits of technology has led to higher usage of manual labour across the logistics industry whether an entry tax on goods coming into a city. The tax is a major source of revenue for city municipal corporations it is in the distribution activities or within plants. Many firms try to compete through the factor advantage of low wages which have necessitated hiring low or no skill personnel thereby sacrificing productivity related gains in the long run.

THE CHANGING LOGISTICS INFRASTRUCTURE

With rising consumer demand and the resulting growth in global trade, the role of infrastructure support in terms of rails, roads, ports and warehouses hold the key to the success of the economy. In this section we provide a quick overview of the status of the logistics infrastructure in India and the current initiatives, both private and public, in that area.

Goods are transported predominantly by road and rail in India. Whereas road transport is controlled by private players, rail transport is handled by the Central Government. With the second largest network in the world, road contributes to 65 per cent of the freight transport (*Rastogi*, 2006). Road is preferred because of its cost effectiveness and flexibility. Rail, on the other hand, is preferred because of containerisation facility and ease in transporting ship-containers and wooden crates. Sea is another complementary mode of transport. Ninety-five per cent of India's foreign trade happens through sea. India has 12 major ports, six each on the West and East coasts and 185 minor ports. Table 2.2 maps the various modes on different performance indicators, clearly indicating the vitality and importance of road transport in Indian economy. There is also evidence of an, across the board, increase in freight traffic for all modes indicating an increased logistics activity. For instance, the percent change in road, rail, air and sea cargo traffic has increased, between 2001 and 2005, from 5 to 14 per cent, 4 to 7.5 per cent, 6 to 20 per cent and 3.5 to 11 per cent respectively (*CMIE Database*, 2006)[11].

Table 2.2. Comparison Chart for Various modes

	Rail	Road	Sea
Number (wagons, trucks, ships)	214760	3487538*	806
Freight Capacity (mn ton)	10.66	5.12*	7.9
Route Length (mn km)/ Number of major ports	0.11	3.34	12
Freight Revenue (US $ bn)	7.00	38.64	4304
Major Products	coal, steel, petroleum, primary metals	automobile, electronic items, garments etc.	iron ore, coal, petroleum (and industrial and consumer products on the out-bound export)

Source : Annual Survey Hindu 2006
*This figure is for 2002-03 1 US$ = Rs 44

In keeping with the increasing demand for road transportation, the National Highway Authority of Indian (NHAI) has been strengthening and widening national highways in multiple phases. As part of the National Highways Development Project, the work on the development of golden quadrilateral (connecting Delhi, Mumbai, Chennai and Kolkata) and the North-South and East-West links were started in 1998. It will build 13000-km expressways that would connect the nation (*Surabhi,* 2006). NHAI is investing about $650mn towards the development of an Intelligent Transportation System (ITS) which will make transport services on the highways (like reducing congestion, advance signaling, medical assistance, accident management, etc.) efficient and automating many processes like toll collection etc. (*Sanjai,* 2007).

Because of the growing opportunity and potential for high revenue, the Ministry of Railways has been taking measures to expand the rail connectivity and recapture the market share of freight business. By focussing on improving wagon utilisation, the Railways have managed to reduce the freight cost from 61 paise 2 per net tonne km (ntkm) in 2001 to 56 paise per ntkm in 2005. At present, goods train run on same railway tracks as passenger trains at an average speed of around 25 kmph. With the proposed dedicated west and east freight corridors, the goods trains are expected to run at 100kmph. The West and East rail corridor of 1469-km and 1232-km will be built with an investment of $2.60 bn and $2.40 bn respectively and will be equipped with the latest centralised traffic control systems. Indian Railways has also decided to collaborate with bulk users of freight transport to build the rail network in a Public Private Partnership (PPP) mode. The first project on this line comprises nine public and private sector companies that are building a 82-km rail line between Haridarpur and Paradip at a cost of $ 120 mn (*Telegraph,* 2006). Recently several steel companies have also shown interest in linking iron and coal mines in Orissa with a 98-km rail line (*Business Standard,* 2006).

Multi-modal transport in India was a monopoly of the Container Corporation of India till 2005. With licences being given to 13 new private players, rail trade should improve considerably. In order to encourage trade by small-scale industries, Indian Railways has started a "road-railer"system where container vehicles are capable of running both on highways hauled by trucks and on rail. In 1998-99, the Konkan Railway (one of the railway zones in South-Western India) pioneered the 'roll-on, roll-off' ('RO-RO') concept between Mumbai (Kolad) and Goa (Verna). Privately owned trucks are loaded with their goods which are driven on to a rake of flat cars and are carried (trucks and their cargo) to the destination.

In 2005-06, the ports handled 456.20 million tonnes of cargo traffic. This is expected to increase to 700 million tonnes by 2011-12. In keeping pace with the growing demand, the government plans to increase port capacities to around 1 billion tonnes per annum in the next six years (*Raja*, 2006). Under the National Maritime Development Programme (NMDP), the government is encouraging public-private partnership to build and maintain ports. This scheme will cover 276 port related projects at an investment of $12.40 bn (*Raja*, 2006). With rising congestion levels at major ports and with high average turnaround time, the government has decided to develop minor ports in seven states to ease the traffic of major ports (*Financial Express*, 2006b).

Table 2.3. Average Turnaround Time At Ports (in Days)

Port	2000-01	2001-02	2002-03	2003-04	2004-05	2005-06	CAGR
Chennai	6.40	5.80	5.30	3.70	4.60	3.80	(9.90)
Cochin	3.23	3.10	2.37	2.19	2.22	2.33	(6.32)
Haldia	5.21	3.96	4.01	3.02	2.87	3.00	(10.45)
Jawaharlal Nehru	1.72	2.48	2.34	2.28	2.04	1.84	1.36
Kandla	6.15	4.72	6.55	5.94	5.06	4.62	(5.56)
Kolkata	6.59	5.50	4.71	4.47	4.29	4.17	(8.75)
Marmugao	4.30	4.25	2.04	3.86	4.47	4.35	0.23
Mumbai	5.60	5.20	5.47	5.06	4.10	4.21	(5.55)
New Mangalore	3.80	2.89	2.73	1.90	2.35	2.96	(4.87)
Paradip	3.89	4.16	3.99	3.37	3.42	3.41	(2.60)
Tuticorin	6.39	4.10	4.11	3.59	2.59	2.66	(16.08)
Vishakhapatnam	4.75	3.71	3.51	3.72	3.33	3.20	(7.60)
Average	4.84	4.16	3.93	3.59	3.45	3.38	(6.92)

Table 2.3 the operational performance of various ports in India—while there is an improvement in performance,

the pace is slow. The estimated cost of this development is expected to be around \$350 mn. Further, private sector is likely to invest \$ 7.67 billion over the next six years.

Currently, fifteen private sector projects are operational at various major ports and four more projects are under implementation. One of them aims to build the deepest port in the world at an investment of \$ 1bn. This project is handled by a three-firm Chinese consortium with a Mumbai-based partner, Zoom Developers. Interestingly, firms like Ambuja Cement have been using barges for transport of clinkers from their factories to crushing and packaging plants all over the coast, thereby, reducing transport costs considerably. It can be seen that there is a fury of activity in enhancing the infrastructure capacities in the country.

DETERMINANTS OF LOGISTICS GROWTH IN INDIA

The Indian logistics business is valued at US\$ 14bn and has been growing at a CAGR of 7-8 per cent. As mentioned earlier, the logistics cost represents 13-14 per cent of the country's GDP. The market is fragmented with thousands of players offering partial services in logistics; it is estimated that there are about 400 firms capable of providing some level of integrated service (*Mahalaksmi*, 2006). The economy is expected to grow around ten per cent over the next ten years and sectors like chemicals, petrochemicals (especially distribution), pharmaceuticals, metals and metal processing, FMCG, textile, retail and automobile are projected to grow the fastest. New business models are emerging as new firms, both domestic and foreign, enter the market. As a result of the ensuing competition, linkages with global supply chains and domestic market growth promise to change the face of logistics industry beyond recognition. In this section, we discuss how these are going to determine the growth of the sector[9].

The scale of operations in manufacturing is changing and so are their markets and sourcing geographies. Growth in manufacturing in India has happened across clusters that are located in different parts of the country, *e. g.,* Ludhiana, NCR, Baddi and Dehradun in North, Rajkot, Jamnagar, Pune and Mumbai in West (along with Ankleshwar, Vapi, Aurangabad, and Kolhapur and most recently Kutch), and Coimbatore, Vishkahpatnam, Bangalore, Hosur, Chennai, Pudduchery and Sriperumbudur in the South. Assembly plants at these locations are being fed with raw materials and intermediate products from all over the country and abroad (as well as these locations). Moreover, distribution networks with emerging hubs in Indore and Nagpur (*i.e.,* Central India) supply all over the country and abroad. This is going to increase the nature and extent of movement of goods and services across the country. This has been accompanied by the expansion of domestic production capacity (*e.g.,* ORPAT in Morbi has added capacity to produce 40, 000 units of quartz clocks and time pieces at a single location) as well as a big MNC entry into the Indian manufacturing scene (*e.g.,* NOKIA's new factory at Sriperumbudur produces 1 million mobile phones per month). As the volume of production grows, so will the extent of movement of goods either to the ports for export or to the rest of the country. Some of the large players to enter (or expand significantly) the Indian market recently have been Reliance Retail, Big Bazaar Hypermart, Pantaloon and RPG in Retail; Nokia, LG, Samsung, Motorola, Sony, Blue Star in Consumer Electronics; Bajaj, Hero Honda, Maruti, Honda, Toyota, Audi, Volkswagen, Renault, Volvo in the Automotive sectors; Holcim in Cement; etc. It can be expected that their operations will drive the growth of logistics industry.

The liberalised Indian economy is experiencing entry of large domestic and global firms in new businesses as well as enlargement of distribution network of many regional Indian firms. The announcement of large retail projects by Reliance and Bharti (in collaboration with Wal-Mart) will bring new technology, add additional warehouse capacity and will require fast and reliable movement of goods across the country. Reliance is thinking of establishing large warehouses in Thailand to take advantage of low cost sourcing from South-East Asia once the Free Trade Agreement with Thailand (as well as ASEAN) gets finalised. Similarly, regional food and grocery retail leaders like Subhiksha who are present very extensively in the South Indian market are now entering the rest of the country with more than 600 new retail stores in 2007. Their logistics strategy and needs are transforming very significantly with this nationwide expansion. New retail chains are entering the non-metro towns and non-State capitals. It may be mentioned that the growth of the courier industry post-liberalization has helped change the parameters of service evaluation in the industry from cost alone to cost, time, and reliability. This sector has also seen a number alliances between regional and local players especially in the small package (less than 500 grams) market thereby creating networks of small players who are not only cost effective but also more flexible than the large national players. This segment of the industry has taken advantage of the large manpower and is gradually moving away from "Angadiyas" or manual inter-city couriers to a more organised network that shares transport infrastructure (and even consolidates sub-packages from various small couriers in a single large courier bag to be transported by air cargo or road transport rather than these sub-packages being carried by several manual couriers on the train; the courier firms are gaining on service and are sharing fixed costs).

The entry of large third party logistics (3PL) carriers like Federal Express and DHL and the expansion of domestic networks of Indian firms like Gati and Shreyas Shipping is also transforming the nature of services and the business practices across the sector. Table 2.4 gives an idea of the investment plans announced by the various firms for the coming financial year and gives a sense of their increasing activity. Another trend driving growth in this sector has been the consolidation amongst the logistics player. Mergers and Acquisitions amongst Indian and MNC logistics firms is starting to increase the reach of MNC 3PLs in the domestic market while consolidating the business (*e.g.*, DHL acquired Blue Dart, TNT acquired Sppedage Express Cargo Service, Fedex bought over Pafex etc.).

Table 2.4. Investment Plans of Major 3PL Service Providers

Firms	Investment Details/Plans (2007-08) (in US $ mn)
DHL	260
TNT	115
Gati	200
*Shreyas Shipping and Logistics	350

Source: Annual Report Hindu 2007.

Consolidation is expected to be beneficial to both the service providers as well as the consumers. Initially MNC 3PL firms were providing only custom clearance and freight forwarding facility to their international clients. With the logistics market growing we should see a shift in this trend. Logistics activity for Nokia's India Hub was maintained by a large number of service providers. Coordination and handover was service providers. Coordination and handover was a problem at times. With DHL acquiring Blue Dart, it is now able to provide seamless end-to-end integrated supply chain solutions. Downstream distribution channels have also seen some consolidation. Manufacturing firms, particularly, in the FMCG sector have started to reduce the number of wholesalers (and at times, distributors) so as to increase the reach and consequently the returns to each wholesaler. This also induces them to invest in new productivity enhancing technology and effective managerial practices. Technology in the logistics chain is being upgraded bringing better visibility on customer off-takes (though an absence of cash registers and the accompanying regulatory discipline to avoid tax evasion stand in the way of automated data updation).

Introduction of more efficient transport technology and mobile communication has the potential of changing the logistics practices in the industry. Increasing competition and the low penetration of IT also implies that the scope for change is immense and imminent. The agri-business sector's supply chain, for example, has changed significantly with increasing investment in cold-chains across the country. With this, fruits and vegetables are being transported long distances (often more than 1500 kms) and milk grid is able to pickup and deliver liquid IMA India Research and Publications milk from and to remote areas more frequently. Here the role of cooperatives like AMUL has been exemplary both in increasing the size of the distribution network and also in re-organizing the supply network very efficiently along with enormous build-up of social capital—a pre-requisite for growth in emerging economies (*Chandra* and *Tirupati*, 2003). Low penetration of hand held technologies for order processing and tracking, product tracking and material handling accessories, as well as IT for improved decision-making can be seen as opportunities for growth. Mobile technologies also hold the potential for rapidly using information for real time decision making as well as for coordinating both the inbound and outbound logistics. Indian customers exhibit strong value and variety seeking behaviour hence developing capabilities in the process of product and service delivery will induce loyalty (*i.e.*, process loyalty).

Government policies have been another driver of change in the logistics industry. The trend towards a higher road cargo traffic as compared to rail is going to require better logistics control and coordination. The golden quadrilateral road project and the east & west rail corridors are expected to change the reactiveness of Indian firms through shorter lead times as well as lower maintenance costs on the transport equipment. They also have the potential of reducing the procedural delays on highways by reducing the number of checks and related stoppages of vehicles. Its impact on perishable good will be most significant. Thirteen States and three UTs have already amended the State laws allowing private sector participation in direct purchases of farm produce from farmers which is making procurement more efficient and is bringing better technology as well as products in the rural production and distribution network (*e.g.*, see ITCe choupal in the next section). Banks have developed venture capital funds for logistics players. Small Industries Development Bank of India or SIDBI, for instance, has invested $ 2.3 mn in the Mumbai based firm Direct Logistics.[10] The unbundling of the logistics supply chain (both the physical pick-up, storage and movement of goods as well as allied services like invoicing, order management, freight forwarding, customs clearance, octroi tax management etc.) will lead to business opportunities and add value to the customers. An interesting example is that of Reliance Connect Service Centres that have been established on Indian highways by Reliance industry along with petrol stations. The Connect Centres provide a place for truckers to relax (sometimes with overnight stay facilities), send information (including data) to parent firms on their location, completed transactions etc., receive material/ instructions from the firm, remit money to parent firm, etc. It has become a one-stop shop for truckers and their companies to keep in touch. Similarly, once VAT is introduced, it will simplify the process of goods servicing and will lead to rationalizing of many operational decisions.

The implication of the emergence of a strong service industry on logistics performance is not well understood. Perhaps, a new business segment will emerge that is technology driven and will help coordinate activities across business channels. For example, there is a need to integrate the flow of information, goods and services between a medical physician, a diagnostics center, hospitals and nursing homes, and retail medical outlets—all of which are un-coordinated independent entities at the moment. This could range from digital transmission of MRI scans from a diagnostics center to a physician's computer to blood collection and delivery from various city centers to nursing homes/blood banks or directly to dispersed operation theatres. The role of a coordinating agency becomes, organisationally, valuable in such an environment. The need is to link physical logistics processes with communication technologies –building on the strengths of the IT and mobile communication industries.

THE RENEWAL OF THE SECTOR: SOME INNOVATIVE EXPERIENCES

There have been several instances of firms undertaking innovative re-design of their logistics systems or deployment of interesting business models to enhance the effectiveness of their networks in order to deliver value to their customers. Sometimes it was done to overcome an inherent disadvantage that may exist in the supply chain. In this section, we present a few such experiences both at the firm level and at the industry level, through brief caselets highlighting their innovative contribution. They also represent the renewal process that is transforming the logistics sector and the distribution strategy of firms.

GATI

Established at a time (in 1989) when firms in India hardly outsourced their logistics requirements, Gati has transformed itself from a cargo movement company to become one of the leading end-to-end logistics and supply chain solutions provider in India. Continuous innovation and high end technological investments to improve service quality, speed and efficiency can be ascribed as the reasons behind their success. It is staring to connect with mass retail market in several cities through 1500 Customer Convenient Centres. It is also the first Indian company to operate in the far-east market with its own subsidiary in Hong Kong. On the service front, there have been several firsts in India by Gati—a money back guarantee on cargo services, cash-on-delivery and a toll-free number for convenience of customers.

Gati operates one of the largest road networks linking 594 districts out of a total of 602 districts in India at a turnover of $104 mn in 2005-2006. It covers 3.2 lakh4-km every day with a fleet size of 2000 trucks. Its automated shipment tracking ability has brought it closer to the customers—for example, the SMS based tracking system has allowed the customers to continuously get an update on the status of their consignment. Another feature also enables customers to get email based conformation of any delivery.

Gati has also transformed the warehouse management practices in India with its modern system, WMS—a web based warehouse management system that provides both functionality and flexibility to customers in managing their warehouse operations. WMS enables Gati and its customers to track inventory status in real time. Along with its transportation related capabilities, this has allowed Gati to manage the entire outbound logistics (*i.e.,* warehousing, transport and dealer/retailer replenishment) of Blue Star for his home air-conditioning division. Order processing times and shipping errors have decreased and customer service levels have improved, as a consequence. Currently, Gati operates with 10 warehouses and plans to setup another 25 over the next three years at an investment of $100mn. It is designing these new warehouses with mechatronic systems that could lead to a paradigm shift in warehouse management in India. It has implemented CRM and ERP systems, using IT to full advantage delivering value to the customers.

AMUL

The Kaira District Milk Cooperative Union or better known as AMUL was established in 1946 in Anand in the western State of Gujarat with an aim to remove the intermediaries in the milk procurement and distribution process and thereby increase return to milk farmers. The milk farmers were mostly marginalised members of the society and most of them barely poured a few litres of milk each day.

1 lakh = 100,000

www.amul.org;

They, however, depended on this for their livelihood and any money lost to the middleman or to uncertainty in the environment meant a threat to their existence. Thus was born AMUL (which means invaluable in Hindi)! The Story of AMUL is an extraordinary story of vision, effort and power of networks for the benefit of the poor. From being a net importer of milk in 1947 when India became independent, India has now emerged as the largest milk producer in the world. This remarkable story has been scripted by a network of cooperatives called AMUL.

The AMUL network is coordinated by the Gujarat Cooperative Milk Marketing Federation (or GCMMF) which markets milk and milk products that are produced by 12 Milk Unions (each having several factories) one of which is AMUL at Anand. The Unions are spread in twelve districts of Gujarat. Each Union collects milk from farmers through cooperative Village Societies. (This structure is now replicated in almost all the States of India.) In 2005-2006, GCMMF had a sales turnover of $860mn through milk and milk products (its Unions or plants produce 15 categories of milk products with several products in each category).

The 12 Unions collect about 6. 3million litres of milk every day from 2.5 million farmers through 11, 962 Village Societies. (with an annual collection of 2.28 bn litres in 2005-2006). Each village society may have 100 to 1000 member farmers who pour milk twice a day. Twice daily, about 500 trucks collect milk from these Village Societies and bring them to either of the five chilling centers or the processing plants (or Unions). The Unions process the liquid milk – produce milk of various types for consumption, convert some to powder as inventory and use both powder and liquid milk for producing milk products. These products are distributed to consumers through a channel comprising 4000 stockists (or distributors) and 5,00,000 retailers. It is not difficult to imagine the complexity of coordinating such a network of perishable products with an explicit social objective, in addition to a commercial one. The network realised the need for a unique model to deliver value to customers and through that serve the key objective of setting up of the cooperative—making a producer out of a poor consumer and helping her get better returns. Briefly, we will illustrate the unique mechanisms used by this network to coordinate the complex supply chain through the intervention of a number of third party service providers (distributors, retailers, logistics service providers and IT support groups). The network practices frequent delivery and works with low inventory levels in the chain, supported by extensive information network and IT kiosks at the milk pick-up locations that provide a variety of services. Payment to farmers for RM procurement is instantaneous (well, almost!) – during the same or in the next pouring shift by the Village Society staff. Milk is carried in cans by trucks (twice daily) or in chilling trucks, once in a day, to the plants. The routes of the trucks are well established and the arrival timetables at each Society well known and rarely is there any delay. This helps provide visibility to every member of the chain and improves the return on investment in the channel. The network operates with a zero stock out through improved availability of products and quick delivery. Disciplined planning to reduce variability at each stage helps in maintaining timeliness in the channel. GCMMF coordinates the production plan between the twelve Unions and ensures matching of geographic markets with supplies. TQM and Hoshin Kanri are the key tools used to plan and implement daily production and change programmes—these have facilitated a six-sigma performance throughout the network and has led to a doubling of sales revenue in the last ten years. Most interestingly, AMUL has the largest market share in every product category that it competes in its competitors are both large MNCs and large and small Indian firms.

AMUL illustrates how good managerial practices can help bridge the gap between profits for the supplier and low cost, highy quality products for consumers—all through exceptional coordination of logistics operations across an extensive network. AMUL operates with one umbrella brand for products from all its member Unions—a testimony to strong quality and cost coordination across all Unions and Village Societies. In addition, its has been singularly responsible for pulling out several million of its members from poverty, ill health and illiteracy through its business model (called Anand Pattern) and social programmes. For details on this case study see Chandra and Tirupati (2003).

THE DABBAWALLAHS OF MUMBAI

The "dabbawallah's" or the 'lunch box delivery people' of Mumbai pick-up and deliver lunch boxes from homes or restaurants and deliver it to the customer's office—all within a specified time frame—and then deliver the empty box back to the place of pick-up. It is an example of how processes can play an important role in coordinating logistics of an important service industry in India. The Nutan Mumbai Tiffin Box Charity Trust of Mumbai was established in 1891 to provide pick-up and delivery of lunch for Britishers working in Mumbai. Since then it has become the leading lunch delivery cooperative in the city. It picks-up and delivers 200,000 lunch boxes in a standard container every day and returns the same to the place of pick-up. The firm has an annual turnover of about $12 mn and employs 5000 people for pick-up and delivery—almost all of them are uneducated. However, there are less than 10 boxes mis-delivered or un-picked in a month! We discuss, briefly, the processes that help make this logistics network error-proof and deliver such an astonishing performance. The operations of the group has attracted global attention and won them many awards. They represent a growing group of service providers that exist as an element of the logistics network, provide niche service and generate value in return for the customer.[12]

The Trust which is organised as a cooperative is operationally organised in hierarchical teams—pick-up teams, consolidation teams, delivery teams (and then the reverse logistics for empty boxes with reversing of the functions for the teams). Typically, each dabba or the lunch box passes through more than four pair of hands and may be transported up to 60-km each way. Pick-up is done between 7.30 am-9.00 am, delivery between 12.00 and 1.00 pm and return between 2.00-5.00 pm. These represent tight time-windows where a team of 20-25 members (and supervised by a team leader who also fills in as a pick-up person in case of any absence) pick-up lunch boxes from homes—about 30 per pick-ups person. The boxes are carried in a specialised fixture on a bicycle to the nearest train station where the boxes are consolidated by destination. A consolidation team performs this task and carries the boxes (which may have been picked by members of different teams but need to travel to the same destination geography) into the train. At the destination station, the lunch boxes coming from various origins/cross-docking destinations, are once again segregated by the building where the delivery is made. Finally, a delivery team picks up their boxes, *i.e.,* boxes that they will deliver to specific owners in specific buildings, carry them on their bicycles and deliver them in the office of the owner of the box. Later in the afternoon, the same person picks-up the empty box and pursues the reverse logistics and the box is ultimately delivered at its point of origin—either a home or a restaurant. With this as the complexity, what may be plausible reasons for such low errors?

Contextually, the group members see their role as very important—they are responsible for delivering food to their customers—socially, it enhances their commitment to their task and establishes a critical customer-service provider link. Operationally, the handoff is done successfully through simplification or breaking down of tasks, codification and repetition. The designed process is simple and easy to understand for each operator. More important, each operator has a limited yet definite role. This role is one of pick-up, consolidation and transfer and delivery (and the similarly for reverse logistics). Each pickup operator does not pick-up more than 25-30 boxes as that is the number of addresses etc. that he can remember accurately which helps in avoiding mistakes. The lunch box is enclosed in a standard container which carries a unique code for the destination station, the building where the box is to be delivered and the floor number in that building where the office of the customer is located. Each operator recognizes a limited set of codes that are relevant to him (and does not have to learn the entire coding scheme). And finally, repetition of the task (i.e., same pickup location, same place for cross docking, same delivery location etc.) helps in making the task foolproof. Of course, what helps is the linear geography of Mumbai, the punctuality of trains, relatively stable demand and strong inter-dependence between operators. It is an example of how manual logistics systems can be organised to effectively deliver value to the customer.

ITC E-CHOUPAL

The e-choupal project was launched by ITC (a large diversified company with strong FMCG presence) in 2000 in the central Indian State of Madhya Pradesh (MP) to re-organise the distribution of soyabean in rural markets. Today e-choupal reaches out to more than 3.5 million farmers in 31,000 villages through 5,200 internet enabled kiosks and now covers a variety of agri-business products. The e-choupal was a unique venture which aimed to eliminate the middlemen from the agricultural commodity supply chain and reduce information asymmetry for the farmers. It is an extremely profitable rural distribution system with its unique design features.

The e-choupal was started with an objective to re-organise the soybean trade which was operating in an inefficient manner. Farmers used to sell their produce through government mandated markets called “mandis”. Mandi trading was conducted by commission agents who bought and sold the produce. As the produce was sold through auction by these traders, farmers would find out the market price only upon arrival at a mandi. If the buyers had purchased enough for the day at this mandi then either the auction prices fell dramatically or the farmers had to wait for the next day's auction. While all this may have been happening at one mandi, the farmers were unaware of the auction status at other mandis where there could have been shortages. The decision regarding the quality of the produce was also dependent on the trader. Similarly, distortions in price and quality effected agro-business trading firms like ITC who were, by government law, required to purchase from the mandi and through these traders and not directly from farmers.

Under the e-choupal model, kiosks were setup in villages providing farmers information in local language on agricultural inputs, best practices in farming, market price realized at various mandi auctions, weather details etc. Nevertheless, it enabled ITC to purchase products directly from farmers (through a change in the law), enhancing quality of products and significant cost reduction (*e.g.*, it saved $5.40 per tonne on soyabean). The e-choupal now has just two service providers in its procurement chain - the sanchalak, a person between the kiosks and the farmers who inspects the produce and based on his assessment of the quality, the price of the commodity is decided (he gets 0.5 per cent commission on the volume sold) and samyojak, a person who manages the ITC warehouses (he gets 1 per cent commission on transactions). Samyojaks also handle much of the logistics at the procurement hub like storage management and transportation from the hub to processing factories.

ITC was able to overcome the hurdles posed by infrastructure inadequacy in villages. It uses solar energy to power the batteries of the computer kiosks and has shifted from dialup connection to satellite based technology (VSAT). Farmers are now able to make informed decisions as they understand the market better leading to higher productivity. Various seed and fertilizer companies are now able to reach wider market with lesser transaction cost. The e-choupal has provided a market for more than 64 companies (to name a few, Monsanto and Nagarjuna Fertilisers). This innovative direct procurement channel is a win-win mechanism for all the involved parties. ITC is now building a rural retail infrastructure on the foundation of the e-choupal network thereby changing the rural distribution landscape.

TRANSFORMING THE AUTO-COMPONENT REPLACEMENT SUPPLY CHAIN

With changing government policies and consumer preferences, the distribution supply chain of Indian companies has been effected significantly. This poses new challenges for various channel partners. We illustrate this transformation process through the lens of the auto component replacement market supply chain and discuss its implications. We surveyed 21 manufacturers and 22 channel members (distributors, wholesalers and retailers) spread equally in Northern and Western clusters of auto component Industry in India for this purpose. The auto component industry produced parts worth $6.7 billion (2004-05) with 57 per cent of the demand coming from the replacement market (ACMA, 2005). Low entry barriers have led to a large number of players in the replacement market. There are about 400 firms in the organised sector and more than 5000 in the unorganised sector. Another feature of this sub-sector is the long duration of ownership of vehicles in India which leads to high requirement of parts. It is also found, anecdotally, that willingness to pay for parts decreases with the length of ownership. This has led to an intense segmentation of the parts market by price.

Pre–1991, this industry was still in a nascent stage. It was characterised by few manufacturers and low demand. Consequently, the distribution network was flat. Availability of spare parts was a key issue with long delivery lead-times and manufacturers sought large order sizes. This also led to the growth of un-branded parts or parts branded by regional producers (often supplied by small firms) in the replacement market. The product was sold chiefly on personal relationship with the buyer; quality, brand and price were not the selling propositions. Maruti Udyog Limited had created a network of suppliers of quality parts for its vehicles. Hero Honda had done the same for its motorcycles.

Post-1991, the liberalisation of the automotive industry led to an entry of many foreign auto players. Because of the impending automobile industry boom and high margins for distributors, the demand for spare auto-parts was expected to grow. The distribution channel was modified with the entry of two more channel members, *i.e.,* wholesalers and semi-wholesalers. The latter were smaller versions of the former and locally oriented.

The period 1994-2007 saw a major transformation of the distribution structure. OEMs started to operate in the replacement market through a parallel supply chain selling parts through their service stations. Additionally, the entry of large number of channel members caused semi-wholesalers to move out of the supply chain—they either moved up the chain to become wholesalers or moved down to become retailers. To strengthen the coordination of this extended supply chain and to buffer against the differential tax structure across states, companies started to operate with Carry and Forwarding Agents (C&FA). Transportation related activities are carried out by all the members of the supply chain. Manufacturers use services of 3PL for transferring their stock to C&FA and distributor locations. But thereafter, the transportation activity is solely managed by channel members themselves.

An analysis of the available IT infrastructure and its usage pattern for all the channel members in our sample survey indicates that there is a high deviation in the usage of IT in the replacement market supply chain. Eighty seven per cent of the sampled firms use an ERP package—most of which is customised and developed locally. The main impediment in the use of a branded packages is the high cost of purchase and implementation. These packages are used to generate sales report, order from suppliers, account for the financial transactions and track the level of inventory at plant and C&FA. Manufacturers order the stock from suppliers mostly through emails. In order to track inventory in the channel, firms also made IT investments both at C&FA and within the firm. Linking the C&FA to the company website enabled firms to check stock status at the C&FA and reduce the order processing and customer response times. Larger firms are also providing a similar setup to their distributors. Since the C&FA is mostly owned and managed by the firms, manufacturers are also able to check the inventory status, dispatching status and customer records. Distributors have invested primarily in computers for keeping track of the inventory and updating accounting details. On the other hand, rest of the channel partners (wholesalers and retailers) don't even own computers. Parts are ordered primarily on the phone. Interestingly, most distributors were found to be following periodic review policy while the rest of the channel members were following continuous review policy because of their low sales volume.

Post 2007, with the implementation of a uniform tax structure across all states, there will be some changes in the way firms operate. The C&FA will, perhaps, become redundant as most manufacturers will prefer to deal directly with distributors. The concept of an exclusive distributor is expected to vanish. It is expected that with the increase in variety of components, distributors might become wholesalers and will stock multiple brands for the same product. Two parallel distribution channels are expected to be in operation– the OEM chain and the non-OEM chain. OEM network will primarily handle the passenger car replacement parts and the non-OEM distribution network will sell parts for Light Commercial Vehicles, Heavy Commercial Vehicles, 2-wheelers and 3-wheelers as the car customer is becoming more brand conscious even while replacing parts which comes along with superior service. Further, we perceive that the more advanced automobiles, Free Trade Agreement with other Asian countries and VAT are going to change the way the replacement market operates. There will be a rationalization of this market in terms of number of firms competing thereby leading to an improvement in quality, delivery time and availability of parts. The size of the firms is expected to increase with an emergence of large national players (in addition to OEMs). This may reduce the number of producers exclusively focusing on the local markets.

CHALLENGES AHEAD

Several challenges remain before the Indian logistics sector and its future success will depend on the ability of the industry to overcome these hurdles. Some of these impediments are at the firm level while others are at the policy level.

At the policy level, the issues of infrastructure and integration of the nation's logistics network remain the two most critical areas that require attention. The growth of infrastructure, since 1991, has been quite extensive (covering a wide geographical area) as well as strategic-linking the key industrial, consumption and transshipment centers. However, some imminent weaknesses need be addressed. Movement beyond the golden quadrilateral is required to bring goods from upcountry production sources to main shipment centers. The rate of growth of expressway has to increase. Poor road conditions increase the vehicle turnover, pushing the operating cost and reducing efficiency. National highways are being upgraded but they account for a meager 2 per cent of the total road network. More importantly, due to non-contiguous development of expressways, truck traffic has to frequently move from the expressway on to old national highways and *vice-versa*. This is inconvenient and is restricting the utilization of the excellent road network that is being developed. The pricing of the toll on these expressways especially for cargo traffic has also been a deterrent to is usage—perhaps, one needs to understand the price elasticity of this demand and develop appropriate price packages for heavy and frequent users. Here, the role of transport technology needs to be mentioned as well. Once the cost of manufacturing multi-axle trucks comes down, it will see higher penetration and consequently lower per unit cost of transportation. Volvo is trying to develop this market but the volumes of high capacity truck continues to be low. The East and West bulk rail transport corridor will divert some traffic from road provided the secondary movement (*i.e.*, from the nearest station to the plant/warehouse) can be minimised and the issue of security of the goods is addressed adequately. Similarly, river navigation in the North and North-Eastern India can pose useful options for cargo movement in hinterland where road congestion is high.

Goods vehicle run only 250-300-km a day in India as compared to 800-1000-km in developed countries. Inter-state check posts, surprise checks and unauthorized hold ups on highways (some due to security reasons while others are to establish the authenticity of the cargo as declared) create bottlenecks. Entry taxes into cities for goods also create procedural bottlenecks. The Motor Vehicles Act and the Motor Transport Workers Act that regulate driver licensing, loading norms etc. and duty hours of drivers respectively require modification to address the quality of services in this sector. Similarly, while the regional permits that allow a truck to ply between certain states come at a lower cost (as compared to a national permit), it limits the flexibility of truckers to convert opportunities. Indian logistics market remains fragmented on these counts and the national market (as well as service) does not appear as one integrated entity. Harmonisation of taxes, procedures and policies across States is required to facilitate a seamless flow of goods and services. For instance, if there was a nation-wide broadband logistics IT-network then a trucker starting in Chennai (in the southern Indian State of Tamilnadu) could file all the papers in Chennai, get all inspections done there and move without interruptions to say, Jammu (in the northern Indian Sate of Jammu and Kashmir). Each state entry point could have access to those papers and they could flag the truck through their check-post as it reached there with no stoppages or delays. Today, it could take anywhere from half hour to few hours to get papers and goods inspected at each check post. The later could be taken care of by having sealed container carriers. Changes in process technology are needed to increase the effectiveness and responsiveness of the transport network.

In privatising the operations of container traffic through rails, new entrants are expected to face serious problems. Because of limited manufacturing capacity for producing wagons, these firms will have to import wagons at high cost. Huge investments in storage capacities near railway stations will also add to their cost (*Bhatt*, 2006). All these factors will increase the entry barriers for the private operators. Moreover, the tariff structure and revenue sharing is still a hindrance for public-private partnership projects to succeed in infrastructure development.

While the use of IT for logistics management is increasing, it is largely limited to large size firms. This represents an opportunity to further improve the decision making abilities across the supply chain and reduce costs further. For instance, order processing and delivery status are two areas that reflect a certain weakness in servicing. With the growth of the IT sector in India, these are clearly areas that can gain from the IT sector's engagement. For example, manufacturing firms can collaborate with the extensive network of call centers for managing order processing and actual integration of order servicing with the physical supply chain. Similarly, there is a role for emergence of a segment (*e.g.*, a service provider) in the logistics chain that manages dispatch information and performs delivery tracking across manufacturers for their customers. Similarly, only a few thousand vehicles out of a total of several millions have tracking system. Truck manufacturers could integrate the tracking technology in its products and IT servicing firms could provide information service on highways tracking movement of vehicles. This would provide information to distribution firms and help track both the consignment as well as the truck better. As of now, the best service is the one provided by Reliance Connect at their petrol pumps on the highways where truckers stop by and call their firms to inform them of there whereabouts. Such service providers become very valuable to tiny and small trucking companies that proliferate the logistics industry and who do not have the wherewithal to either install or operate their own IT systems. As the concentration in the industry increases, the need to manage larger number of trucks, routes, warehouses and customers will require decision support systems that perform dynamic planning and scheduling. The IT base is indeed low and firms need to compete on the basis of real logistics costs instead of clever accounting practices before the sector will see increased IT penetration. As the need to have visibility in the supply chain increases, better technology applications will also appear.

Another area that will see tremendous growth is outsourcing of logistics service. While logistics outsourcing has been in existence for several decades, it was limited to transportation and warehousing. Post-liberalisation, the country has seen outsourcing of value add services like freight forwarding, fleet management, import/export and customs clearance, order fulfillment, consulting services like distribution network planning etc. These are early years for the 3PL service providers and a recent survey cites lack of trust and awareness as the key hurdles to its growth. Service tax on outsourced cost and the requirement to establish multiple warehousing facilities in order to avoid double taxation (and thereby lose the advantage of scale economies with fewer warehouses) were also found to undermine the 3PL business. According to this survey, most of the 3PL service providers offer limited services. In future, their role as coordinators will require that they offer a wider menu of value add services. They also have the potential of integrating

SME channels through a variety of logistics services and technology across a network of small producers.

The logistics industry is evolving rapidly and it is the interplay of infrastructure, technology and new types of service providers that will define whether the industry is able to help its customers reduce their logistics costs and provide effective service. Changing government policies on taxation and regulation of service providers will also play an important role in this process. Coordination across various government agencies require approval from multiple ministries and is a road block for multi modal transport in India (*e.g.*, ports, roads, railways, container freight operations etc. are all managed by different ministries in the Government of India. At the firm level, the logistics focus will have to move towards reducing cycle times in order to add value to their customers. These are few of the issues one need to take account before the logistics industry can boom significantly in India.

REFERENCES

1. *Logistics Management*—Indian Edition by Reed Infomedia India, Vol. 1, Issue 4, July 2007.
2. *Cargo Times*, Vol. 7, Issue 5, July 2007.
3. *Cargo Times*, Vol. 7, Issue 5, July 2007.
4. *Survey of Indian Industry* 2007—The Annual Hindu Publication.
5. *Logistics Management*—Indian Edition by Reed Infomedia India, Vol. 1, Issue 1, April 2007.
6. *www.economywatch.com*
7. *Cell News Letter* Oct., 2007.
8. Srinivasan, G(2006) "Public-Private Partnership is the Way to Build Infrastructure", *Hindu Business Line*, 7 October, 2007.
9. Logistics : The Next Big Growth Driver Article by V. Shunmugum & Ritambhara Singh—*Business Line*, Saturday, March 29, 2008, p. 8.
10. Rastogi, A. (2006) "*Indian Infrastructure Report*", Oxford University Press, 9-12.
11. CMIE Database 2006 on Logistics and Transportation.
12. Chandra, P. (2003) "*Coordinating the Dabbawallah Supply Chain*", mimeo, IIM, Ahemedabad.

Research Methodology

Chapter 3

The main objective of this chapter is to present a detailed account of the importance of the study, steps followed in perusing research, data collection technique, presentation of data and analytical tools used in the analysis.

STATEMENT OF THE PROBLEM

Curiosity or inquisitiveness is a distinctive feature of human beings. Curiosity to know about ourselves, our institutions, our environment, our planet, other planets, and the universe is inherent in us. Innumerable questions go on arising in our mind: what are remedies? What is the shape of the earth? How do solar and lunar eclipses arise?[1]

Research simply means a search for facts—answers to questions and solutions to problem. It is a purposive investigation. It is an "Organised inquiry." It seeks to find explanations to unexplained phenomenon, to clarify the doubtful propositions and to correct the misconceived facts.

In lieu of various issues, the main objective of the present study is to understand the conceptual framework of logistics management, examine its practices in India. It also specifically study to find the role of Container Corporation of India in facilitating logistics and containerisation in the country and examining the system provided by it to enhance trade and activities in the recent years.

OBJECTIVES OF THE STUDY

(*i*) To understand the concept of logistics management its theories and role in international and domestic trade.

(*ii*) To examine the practices of logistics management in India.

(*iii*) To study the role of container corporation of India in logistics management of the country.

(*iv*) To examine the systems provided by container corporation of India to enhance business trade and activities in the recent years.

RESEARCH DESIGN

Research is a scientific endeavour. It involves scientific method. "The scientific method is a systematic step by step procedure following the logical processes of reasoning. Scientific method is a means for gaining knowledge of the universe. As Karl Pearson emphasises "the scientific method is one and same in all branches and that method of all logically trained minds... the unity of all sciences consists alone in their method not in their materials.[2] Although any typology of research is inevitably arbitrary, Research may be classified crudely according to its major intent or the methods. According to the intent, research may be classified as:

- Exploratory Research
- Descriptive Study
- Diagnostic Study

According to the methods of study, research may be classified as:

- Experimental Research
- Analytical Study

The present study is a descriptive and diagnostic study.

Descriptive Research

Descriptive study is a fact-finding investigation with adequate interpretation. It is the simplest type of research. It is more specific than an exploratory study, as it has focus on particular aspects or dimensions of the problem studies. It is designed to gather descriptive information and provides information for formulating more sophisticated studies.

Criteria : All problems do not lend themselves to descriptive study. This method is applicable to problems, which satisfy certain criteria. First, the problem must be describable and not arguable. For instance, philosophical and controversial issues are not suitable for descriptive study. Second, the data should be amenable to an accurate, objective, and, if possible, quantitative assemblage for reliability and significance. Third, it should be possible to develop valid standards of comparison; last, it should lend itself to verifiable procedure of collection and analysis of data.

DATA COLLECTION

The search for answers to research questions is called collection of data. Data are facts, and other relevant materials, past and present, serving as bases for study and analyses. Some example of data is:

Types of data : The data needed for a social science research may be broadly classified into: (*a*) Data pertaining to human beings; (*b*) data relating to organizations; and (*c*) data pertaining to territorial areas.

1. ***Demographic and socio-economic charac-teristics of individuals :*** Age, sex, race, social class, religion, martial status, education, occupation, income, family size, location of the household, life style, etc.

2. ***Behavioural variables :*** Attitudes, opinions, aware-ness, knowledge, practice intentions, etc. Organisational data

consist of data relating to an organisation's origin, ownership, objectives, resources, functions, performance and growth.

Field Visit

For the purpose of developing an understanding of various aspects of CONCOR operations filed visit has been undertaken to various strategic points of importance during the research duration, for instance personal visit has been arranged to Head office of CONCOR in New Delhi, Inland Container Depot. Tuglakabad, Madhosingh, Port Vist to Kolkata Port Trust's Haldia Sea port. The researcher has met numerous key officials; in these institutions of strategic importance and indulged with in valuable discussion regarding the current state of logistics management practices on India. These visits have given valuable practical inputs to the researcher regarding the overall operation aspects of logistics management with special focus on CONCOR. As theory without practical is meaningless and practical without the theory is blank. So a judicious approach has been adopted to develop an understanding of the research problem.

Secondary Data

The secondary sources consists of readily available compendia and already compiled statistical statements and reports whose data may be used by researches for their studies, *e.g.,* Annual survey report, The Hindu, CII Logistics e newsletter, Cargo Times, Logistics Management, Business India, Annual report of CONCOR, Journal of Rail Transport, IRT Manual, Economic Times, Business Line, Statistical statements, Reports of Governments Departments, Annual Reports on currency and finance published by the Reserve Bank of India, Statistical Statements relating to logistics management etc.

Features of Secondary Sources

Though secondary sources are diverse and consist of all sorts of materials, they have certain common characteristics:

First, they are readymade and readily available, and do not require the trouble of constructing tools and administering them.

Second, they consist of data over which a researcher has no original control over collection and classification. Both the form and the content of secondary sources are shaped by other. Clearly, this is a feature which can limit the research value of secondary sources.

CASE STUDY

Case study method has been adopted to pursue the research as in case study requires an in depth study of the subject matter regarding all the minute aspects ranging form strategic importance to tactical needs. So a detailed case study has been undertaken of Container Corporation of India to underline the importance of logistics management practices in India. A case study is an in-depth comprehensive study of a person, a social group, an episode, a process, a situation, a programme, a community, an institution or any other social unit. It is one of the most popular types of research methods. Its purpose may be to understand the life cycle of the unit under study of the interaction between factors that explain the present status or the development over a period of time. Some examples of a case study are: a social-anthropological study of a rural or tribal community; a causative study of a successful cooperative society; a study of the financial health of a business undertaking; a study of labour participation in management in a particular enterprise; a study of juvenile delinquency; a study of life-style of working women; a study of slum dwellers; a study of urban poor; a study of economic offenses; a study of refugees from another country.

ANALYSIS AND INTERPRETATION

Data analysis incorporates various statistical tools depending upon the requirement and necessity of the research problem. In this research problem I had used six years of data from 2001 to 2007 (As this duration covers almost one economic cycle) and for the purpose of analysis following techniques were used: percentage analysis, trend analysis, pie charts, bar diagrams, line diagrams etc. for the purpose of analysis and interpretation.

Findings and Suggestions

Last but not the least was findings and suggestions which were made on the basis of analysis and interpretation. In this particular research study various findings and suggestions are made on the basis of concrete data.

Limitations of the Study

Since there are a lot of logistics companies operating worldwide, the study is focused to only one organization as it is a case study. Other logistics companies are not considered just to ensure a generalised approach. Only published secondary data is considered so unpublished sources are not considered irrespective of their significance, impact or usefulness. Though maximum care has been taken for analyzing the facts and figures even then some amount of human error may remain by chance.

LITERATURE REVIEW

The review of literature is not mere reading for rereading sake; it is also not a causal reading like reading of a story or novel. It is focused and directed towards specific purpose. It is also selective. A researcher has to select the kinds of literature to be reviewed and determine the purposes for which he has to study them. Knowledge is growing rapidly. It gets doubled in a very short span of time. Scholars, researchers and writers go on adding knowledge through their studies and writing.

Prof. Pramod Rao and Kalyani Gohokar have emphasised the importance of effective logistics management in their book which is a humble effort to portray logistics as an agent of change. It explains the contemporary issues and trends in logistics management and how they can be used by corporations to gain strategic advantage. The book endeavors to identify the bottlenecks prevailing in the logistics industry and how solutions are mitigating these problems and accelerating growth for individual countries and globally at large. The book focuses on emerging practices and trends with respect to outsourcing (3PL, 4PL), integration, collaborative and advanced logistics. It includes the impact of geographical and cultural diversities on logistics operations of global companies. It emphasises logistical customer service, and explains how companies balance the effect of increased cost and changing customer preferences. With the help of some articles and examples mentioned in this book, an effort has been made to drive home the point that logistics management can act as a change agent by providing revenue growth and responsiveness making the firm more efficient and profitable. It is hoped that the book will be of great value to organisations, if the logistics management is used as a tool for business strategy.

A Case Study has also been developed on logistics management practices at macro level by Mumbai dabbawalas. Dabbawallahs of Mumbai need no introduction to students, faculty and practitioners of Business Management. It is a business that has lasted over 113 years and is still being run successfully by a group of people with practically no formal education, no investment, and no technology. Management guru C K Prahlad has hailed Mumbai's ubiquitous Dabbawallahs as the quintessential masters of supply chain management. The Dabbawallahs have received attention and prominence in the business world across the globe, having found their way into the Guinness Book of World Records, Ripley's Believe it or Not; documentaries on them have been filmed by the BBC and Discovery Channels; case-studies on their supply chain management capabilities have been developed by the Harvard and Ivey Schools of Business; they have presented Seminars at prestigious leadership summits both at home and abroad; they are the recipients of the Six-Sigma efficiency rating accorded by the Forbes-Global Magazine in 1998, and, they were the only two average Indians to be invited to the Charles-Camilla Royal wedding. The ICBR team is writing a book on the Dabbawallahs, the contents of which will span their 100+ year old history, their impeccable logistics and supply chain management, their business efficiency, their fame, and their future in this rapidly changing world of business. A personal interview with Sri Medge and Sri Talekar has also featured in the book along with a series of photographs and exhibits. Although there have been numerous case studies and articles on the Dabbawallahs, no book on them has been written as yet, thereby making this book the first of its kind.

In his book on Distribution and logistics management Prof. D K Agrawal identified that contemporary philosophy of distribution management has evolved from a 'dark continent of marketing' to a 'strategic tool of marketing' for gaining differential advantage in the hyper-competitive marketplace mainly driven by globalization and information technology. To exploit the strategic competency of distribution management, it is essential to have an integration of logistics with distribution system. Most of the texts available presently on these subjects lack this integrated approach. In this book, an attempt has been made to bridge this gap. Salient features Integration of logistics systems with distribution management in strategic marketing perspectives. Enrichment of knowledge about distribution and logistics management in the information technology perspective. Highlighting strategic role of integrated distribution management for growth and long-term performance of physical product industries. Illustration of conceptual frameworks with best practices and contemporary case studies.

REFERENCES

1. *Methodology of Research in Social Sciences* by OR Krishnaswami and M.Ranganatham, Himalaya Publishing House,New Delhi, 2004.
2. *Statistical Methods* by SP Gupta—Sultan Chand Books, New Delhi, 2004.

Chapter 4

Conceptual Bases of CONCOR

INTRODUCTION

Considering the vast potential in the field of logistics, the Government of India approached rationally in order to provide business activities boon in the country, it created a new logistics organisation Container Corporation of India (CONCOR) before liberalisation era.

Container Corporation of India was incorporated in March 1988 under the Companies Act, and commenced its operation from November 1989 taking over the existing network of 7 ICDs from the Indian Railways. The company was set up with the objective of developing multimodal logistics support for India's International and Domestic containerised cargo[1]. CONCOR's main strength can be characterised as:

- Relatively undisputed position 'as sole provider of rail hauls for containers'.
- Ability to provide modal choice. (Road or rail or air) according to the needs of the shipper and lead from the port.
- Strong relationships with Indian Railways.
- Sole provider of containerised rail transport in India.

- Financial figures of CONCOR for the last ten years show a positive trend turnover registered a steady increase from Rs. 500 million in 1991-92 to Rs. 128646 million in 2001-02.

Evaluating the role played by CONCOR is improving the country's logistics system; it needs a more focussed study. Especially when the Indian business markets are open and facing stiff competition from the systematic logistics pattern followed by the foreign companies while starting their operation in our country.

Before discussing in detail about the CONCOR, researcher would like to explore the bases of CONCOR.

Without discussing the elements of transportation, multimodal transport, Warehouse and containerisation, the study on CONCOR under logistics management practices would be inappropriate.

TRANSPORTATION

The climax of 'transport industry' is not a more movement of persons and goods from one place to another but the real excitement incorporates the overall growth and development of civilisation in general and economy in particular. The essential prerequisite for the rapid growth and development of any progressive economy is the existence of an adequate infrastructure which generally incorporates energy, transport and communication. In other words, infrastructure is of great importance for the working of an economy *e.g.* natural resource like men and materials become productive, if and only if, they are transported from the place of origin to the place of utilisation.

Similarly, the success or failure of any business activity is largely dependent on the final travel outputs from the point of production to the point of final consumption at an economy of scale.

The Indian economy is generally characterised by a wide coverage of the geographical area, extensive coastlines, large population as well as abundance of mines, minerals along with agricultural lands. It needs a variety of transport facilities in adequate quantities. There are a lot of transport benefits to an economy, mainly divided in two broad categories, namely, economy and non-economic.[2]

Economic Benefit Includes

Transportation make products available to the final condemns *i.e.* it serves not only existing demands, but also stimulates new demands by extending the variety of goods that can be made available anywhere and everywhere.

- It facilitates production by moving different means of production, *i.e.* raw materials, machines, tools, men, etc. to places of production where these are best suited. Transport also encourages regional specialisation for competitive advantages.
- It is also considered as a key agency for the promotion of planned development *i.e.* regional economic disparities can be removed by way of transport.
- Transport provides ample opportunity for acceleration of employment and income, which in turn, create demand for consumer goods.

Non-economic benefits of transport may be judged by its great contribution towards social, political as well as cultural integration of mass population of any country with different moods, languages, castes, creed and traditions.

Due to the above mentioned economic and non-economic benefits associated with transportation, are available in our country, namely, air, road, rail, water and pipeline transport.

Although, relative advantages and disadvantages are associated with each transport system in terms of costs, damages in transit, speed, reliable timely delivery, specialised facilities and accessibility. That is why firms have different preference choice pattern for different purposes.

Position of Transportation in Logistics Management

Transportation is the main oratory of logistics. It refers to the movement of goods from one location to another. The very mission of logistics is to make available the right quantity of the right quality of goods at the right time and place at least cost. This can be achieved by the proper planning of movement of goods and appropriate use of transportation goods.

Normally, the share of transportation cost is about 40 per cent of the total logistical costs. Hence, any effort to cut down the logistical costs needs efficient and effective utilisation of transportation facilities and its trade off with other logistical components.

Being an integral part of total logistics and supply chain system in India, railways and roadways carry about entire domestic freight cargo, where as sea ways and airways for international freight cargo.

At the advent of growing awareness regarding the overwhelming contribution of logistics and supply chain management for sustainable growth and core competency, expectation of corporate world from transportation industry is increasing significantly due to the prevailing global competitive environmental scenario, corporate enterprises are continuously under pressure to cut down logistical cost and improve customer service capabilities. That is why, they need :

- Reduction in transit time for minimisation of inventory cost;
- Less damages, en-route handling and pilferage for minimum insurance charges;
- Curtailment of protective packaging costs; and
- Point-to-point information regarding the status of the shipment.[3]

In fact, the transportation services have become more imperative due to the logistical approach for speedier and timely delivery of goods, economies in operation, minimum en-route handling and documentation to minimise transportation cost and particularly total logistical costs.

The service portfolio of transport industry normally required by the corporate enterprises includes committed timely delivery, express cargo management, multi modal transportation, warehousing, inventory management, protective packaging , money collection and management container truckload, door to door delivery, coastal shipping, clearing and forwarding in the case of international shipment, bar coding, electronic data interchange, total insurance and risk management, value added service, material handling and emergency services. In other words, it can be said that now-a-days, corporate enterprises need a total movement solution under one roof with state of the art transport technology.

Liberalisation, privatisation and globalisation have further increased the market scope, where the world market is shrinking into a global village. In this situation, movement of goods and products has become move imperative and also wider. Transportation has a significant link with various stages of global supply chain.

Thus, the success of any logistical system and coordinated and efficient supply chain performance, transportation plays a very strategic role because:

- In ensures speedier and timely physical movement of goods from point of inception to the point of consumption;
- It creates core competency by preventing stock-out and customer annoyance;
- It provides protective storage during transit;
- It ensures cost efficient better customer service;
- It fulfils specific service requirements of the corporate enterprises for improvement of logistical capabilities and harmonious supply chain relationships.

Element of Transportation Cost

It has already been said that transportation cost is one of major constitutes of total logistical costs. Hence, it is essential to have a proper analysis of transportation costs, which includes various elements. Some elements behave in a contradictory manner with others. For instance, if we opt for a more speedier mode of transportation, say airways, the transit time, obsolescence and deterioration costs are less but tariff cost goes up.

Following are the various elements of transportation cost:

Tariff of Transport Mode : These elements of transportation refers to freight charge of various modes of transport to be paid for movement of goods from one location to another. Tariff of airways is highest, followed roadways, railways, sea ways and pipelines.

Normally, freight charge increases with the decrease in transit time, *i.e.* higher the transit time, lower the freight cost. Tariff of transport mode largely depends upon a large number of factors such as nature of the product, distance to be covered, volume/quantity to be shipped, density (weight and space) of the product, en-route handling requirements, value-added service requirement of the shipper, shipper-carrier contract and trade relationships etc.

Transit Time Cost : This cost of transportation deals with the cost of inventory in transit. From total logistics costs point of view, this element of transports costs is very significant. If the transit time of particular mode of transport is longer, it means that the product of the company remains in transit for a longer period of time. So, the involvement of working capital is for a longer period of time, resulting into higher transit time costs.

Obsolescence and Deterioration Cost : These elements of transport cost involve costs caused due to deterioration and obsolescence in the physical attributes of the product during transit. There are certain categories of products which are perishable and delicate in nature, whose physical attributes deteriorate over a period of time, gradually resulting into devaluation of the product.

For instance, fish is transported from Andhra Pradesh to most of the country, any delay in transit forces the marketers to sell them at a less-than-desired price. Hence this cost comes under transportation expenses as obsolescence and deterioration costs.

Protective Packaging Cost : For specific products and modes of transport, there is requirement of specific protective packaging. Hence, such a cost comes under total transport costs. For instance, if a product is shipped by railways, more sophisticated protective packaging is required to protect goods from breakages and pilferages.

Transit Insurance Cost : Transit insurance cost, another element of transport cost, is the cost of insurance paid to insurance company to cover various types of risk. At the advent of containerisation, this cost has been minimised due to lesser chances of damages of goods during transit.

Miscellaneous Costs : Apart from the above elements of transport costs, there are other miscellaneous costs, such as local taxes, octroi etc.

WAREHOUSING

Storage is an economic convenience rather than a necessity in the logistics system. As one analyst puts it, storage is "little more than transportation at zero miles an hour". It is simply a static accumulation of inventory for a period of time. Storage activity can be separated from inventory, material handling and warehousing functions. Inventory is an activity concerned with tracing the product's flow through a typical warehouse. Material handling relates to the activates of loading and unloading, moving a product to and from various locations within the warehouse and order picking. On the other hand, concept includes the storage and retrieval operations, the organizational aspects, the mechanisation of equipment for material handling, media for material storage and the building itself, which is essential to protect the goods environment. This chapter deals with warehouse management activity centre of logistics.

WAREHOUSING DEFINED

Both the physical processes of material handling and stocking, as well as the underlying methodologies, are commonly denoted by the word 'warehousing'. A warehouse can be defined as a planned space for the efficient accommodation and handling of goods and materials.[4]

Roos has further defined warehousing as the segment of an enterprise's logistics function that is responsible for storage and handling of inventories. The management of this process includes the maintenance of accurate and timely information relating to the status, location, condition and disbursement of inventory.

As clear from the above definitions warehouses are needed:

1. To provide an adequate buffer storage against inequalities caused by unpredictable variation in supply and demand. This helps a company to guard against loss of production, to ensure production in economic batch sizes, to provide marketing back up by maintaining the availability of spares and adequate service levels and at times to provide a speculative hedge against anticipated inflation;
2. To safeguard stock from damage, deterioration and unauthorised removal by providing an environment which is appropriate to the material being stored;

3. To record accurately receipts, stock holding and dispatches and to provide an efficient communicational interface with all appropriate parts of the system that are being served.

In addition, an efficient system can present in image, which if properly exploited, can greatly enhance a company's goodwill. Many a time, this factor alone is the determining factor in the choice of a warehouse. The important fact to remember here is that all these functions have to be performed by the warehouse at a minimum cost to the total logistics system. Moreover, these functions help us to conclude that warehouse is the interface area for production, market, customer and suppliers.

Thus we are progressively moving away from the generally accepted concept of warehousing *i.e.,* it deals with static storage of goods only. The change in attitude and set of mind led to changing semantic *i.e.,* warehouse to distribution centre. Distribution centre thus is:

- Special kind of warehouse designed to speed the flow of goods and avoid unnecessary storing costs;
- Speeds bulk-breaking to reduce inventory carrying costs;
- Helps to centralise control and co-ordination of logistics activates;
- Products many immediately move (cross-dock) from a truck or train at an incoming loading dock to an outgoing loading dock.

Static storage does not ensure achievement of a management's logistics objective. A complex set of activities or function have to be performed to ensure success in the area of warehousing.

FUNCTIONS OF WAREHOUSES

Warehouses perform a number of functions to ensure that the organisation succeed in fulfilling its objectives.

According to Lamber and Stock warehousing has four basic function (Fig. 4.1) *i.e.,*

(*a*) Material handling

(*b*) Storage

(*c*) Information transfer

(*d*) Customer service

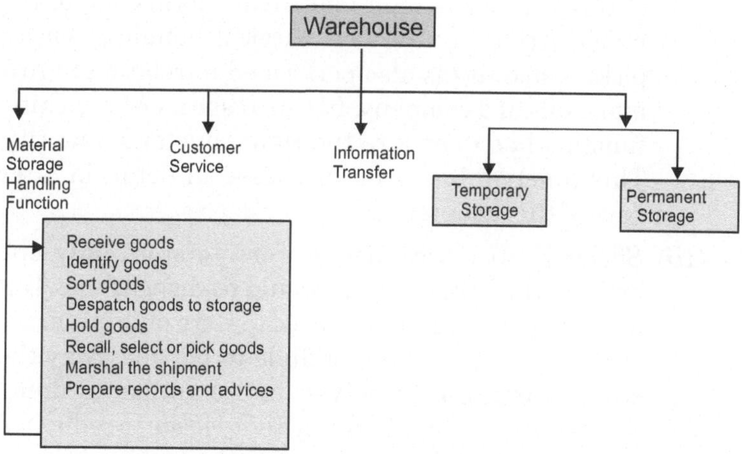

Fig. 4.1. Functions of warehousing

Material Handling Function

It is a broad category which includes a wide array of activities. These are:

(*i*) ***Receiving, storing and shipping :*** Receiving refers to physical order acceptance. This includes audit. Storing deals with putting away received inventory in such a manner that it compliments the order picking activity. Shipping in another activity which comes under this category. It deals with the performing task relating to dispatching of an order. These tasks vary from order consolidation to packaging to transportation dispatching.

(*ii*) ***Order picking :*** Once the inventory is received, the storage function is carried out by putting the goods in proper location and format. Order picking refers to physical selection of products, from their locations, on receipt of a customer order. Orders are picked with the help of a document called pick List. This document contains details like:

These details help meet the customer orders efficiently. But as this activity deals with small volumes, the cost of this activity is high and thus it forms one of the major activity centers of material handling. Order picking activity is also performed in relation to raw materials of a company. In this respect order picking function has to ensure the right time and quantity. This function has been discussed in detail in later part of this chapter.

(*iii*) ***Sorting :*** If a warehouse were to store only one product than this activity would be dispensable. But practically a warehouse is used to store multiple array of products. Thus, in a prelude to putting away the stock, sorting of received merchandise is done. Increased efficiency in this activity leads to reduction in the chances of error during order picking.

(*iv*) ***Traffic management :*** If a company has separate transportation or traffic management department, then a warehouse manager is simply supposed to co-operate and co-ordinate his efforts with this department in choosing the best mode of transport for inflow and outflow of goods. But if there is no separate department then the warehouse manager is required to analyse the carriers suitable for a product shipment, so as to increase customer satisfaction but decrease total transportation cost.

Storage Function

The second function of warehousing is storage. Companies possess warehouse storage space for several reasons. As discussed earlier, a company may opt for warehouse to exploit economies arising as a result of trade-off between the cost of transportation against cost of carrying inventories, to balance sources of supply and demand and to assist in the production process. Warehousing storage function also, in case of certain products, helps in value addition. For example, products like wine, cheese and liquor need to be aged before they can be sold in the market. Storage helps in the ageing process of these products and thus adds value to them. Thus storage function performs the following activities:

1. ***Stock piling :*** This activity refers to the storing of products and materials so as to allow a company to exploit economies in production, and transportation (by allowing the company to transport goods in full truckloads).
2. ***Product rotation :*** In the case of products like wine, cheese and liquor it is essential to have a system where the products which have been properly processed are shipped off to the market, while the new ones are stored for processing. This function ensures that proper value addition takes place in products but at the same time there is minimum loss from obsolescence and spoilage.
3. ***Consolidation and breaking of bulk :*** Distributors require product from the manufacturer proportional to the demand in the market. Usually these are small quantities which constitute less than full truckload. If the quantities were to be shipped as and when the order were received the transportation costs incurred would be fairly high. To overcome this problem a manufacturer convents many small shipments into full carloads, and then ships them to a local or a regional consolidation centre. At these centers the bulk is broken down according to order specifications of individual distributors and this activity is called as the bulk breaking function.

Therefore, the main objective of warehouse storage function is to maximise customer service the efficiency of storage can be estimated by weighing trade-off of warehouse in cost and transportation cost.[5]

Information Transfer Function

The third category of function performed by warehousing is information transfer. In a warehouse, irrespective of how small or large an activity is, details there of are maintained in a record by activates of bookkeeping, stocktaking and control. These records are later used to calculate space utilisation, equipment and manpower availability, throughput time order picking time and efficiency of various other activates. Without timely and accurate information, the companies cannot even think of achieving its sales, marketing or customer service objectives. Thus, information transfer though considered a secondary function of warehousing, is yet an important one.

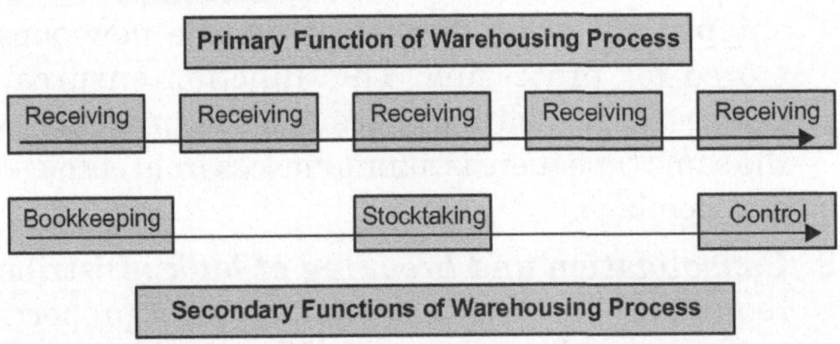

Fig. 4.2. Primary and secondary Function of Warehousing

Customer Service Function

Customer service has been a 'catch all' term used by industry for all critical elements necessary for satisfying customers relative to the firm's present methods of operation. In broad terms, customer service can be considered as the measure of how well the logistics system is performing in creating time and place utility for products, including post sales support. Observed that customers often expect service to be as much a part of a product as are the product design, quality and price. Customer service is also seen as related to aspects of inventory movement and storage, including acquisition of raw materials, co-ordination of work in process inventory, and ultimately, delivery of finished goods inventory.

Traditionally, warehouses were seen as ways of saving money, mainly through reduction in transportation costs. This old relationship has long since changed, and warehouses today are justified as the front line of the firms marketing strategy.

If all these functions incurred zero cost, the dreams of the organisations would be at an arm's stretch. Practically all these functions are performed at a cost. This makes the understanding of warehousing cost essential.

WAREHOUSING COSTS

The warehousing costs are primarily associated with:

- land : Rental costs
- buildings : rents and rates
- storage and materials handling equipment : maintenance
- services : electricity, telephone
- labour : pickers, packers
- supervision : warehouse management
- consumable : materials

Depot costs demand primarily on the volume and nature of the throughput, together with the storage and handling methods employed. In addition to above factors warehousing costs are influenced by location and the number of warehouses. In this section of the chapter, firstly, we will discuss the nature of warehousing costs and then understand the relationship of warehousing cost with that of transportation cost and total distribution costs. Broad classification of costs has been outlined in:

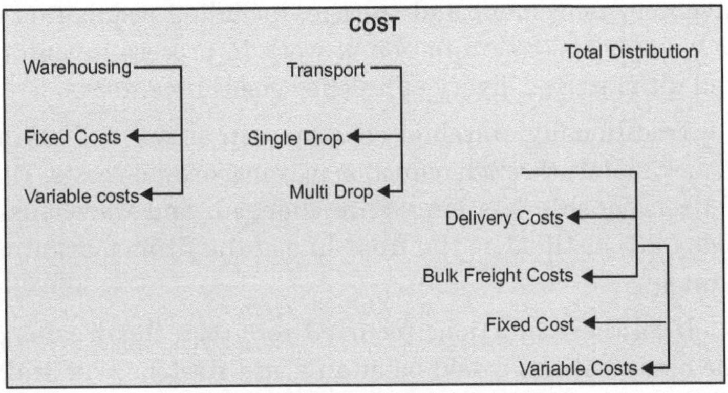

Fig. 4.3. Different Warehouse Cost

WAREHOUSE LOCATION

One of the most heavily explored and refined areas in logistics management are determining warehouse location. During the past few years a lot of effort has been directed into developing complex economic techniques to efficiently determine the location of a warehouse. The location of a warehouse depends upon the characteristics of the firm in questions, like the distribution channel, the resources a company has, the customer service level etc. Depending upon these variables a company can opt for either of the three locations *i.e,* Market oriented warehouse aid to be a warehouse which is located near to the target market or customers. This facilitates:

(*a*) Short delivery movements;

(*b*) Speed of service to the customer.

Thus in the food industry, speed of delivery to the market determines the quality and this in turn the sales of the product.

Production oriented said to be a warehouse which is nearer to the production point, and only after processing the goods are shipped. This facilitates:

(*a*) Economies in transportation costs;

(*b*) The products once received in production-oriented warehouses are then shipped in assorted lots to retailers.

Examples of such warehouses would be agro-processing and steel industries.

Intermediately oriented due to various distribution patterns possible a warehouse can be positioned almost at any point in the distribution channel. The two extremes possible are market oriented warehouse or production-oriented warehouse. But a company depending upon its resources can sometimes opt for intermediately oriented warehouse. These warehouses not only service the market by decreasing the lead time but also provide the facility of economies of transport costs.

In order to locate a warehouse at the most optimum position we should consider two scenarios *i.e.,* single depot location or multiple depot location.

TYPES OF WAREHOUSE

There are several types of are housing alternatives that organisations can pursue. Choosing the appropriate type of warehouse consists of matrix of financial, organisational and legal decisions. The object is to select a type that provides the firm with the ability to achieve the least total cost necessary to efficiently and effectively execute logistics functions while facilitating attainment of enterprise strategic performance targets. The optimal warehouse decisions should permit the firm to leverage inventory levels and transportation models that effectively support marketing, sales order processing and inventory planning in quest for competitive advantage.

The warehouses can be categorised into categories/types on various variables.

On the Basis of Ownership

(*a*) Company owned warehouses

(*b*) Public warehouses

Table 4.1. Difference between Public and Private Warehouses

Characteristics	Private	Public
1. Definition	Private bonded ware-houses are owned and operated by private companies and the private company is the ware-house-keeper. The ware-houses-keeper only bring his own merchandise into this type of warehouses.	These are like the private warehouses except the warehouse and the warehouse-keeper permit other companies to store their goods in the warehouse.
2. Degree of control	Hid degree of control.	Lesser degree of control.
3. Title of ownership	Title of ownership of the warehouse and the goods is with the same company.	Title of ownership of the warehouse and the goods are with different parties.
4. Level of flexibility	Lesser degree of flexibility.	High degree of flexibility. The company has the option of changing the location to gain strategic leverage.
5. Information feedback	The information feedback is more effective as the non company portion in this pipeline is shorter. This is so because the company can control status of the product till it is accepted by a transport carrier.	The information feed-back is less effective as the non company portion in this pipeline is longer.
6. Preferred when company in involved in	• Mall production. • Full time storage capacity is required. • Substantial material handling activities are required	• Making inefficient transport *i.e.*, it is transporting LTL over long distance. • Seasonal storage is required. A product with high degree of demand variance.
7. Geographic location	Concentrated, stable	Dispersed, shifting
8. Level of demand	Stable	Volatile
9. Physical Characteristics of product line	Requires special handling or storage	Standardised packaging, handling and storage.
10. Technique used for transportation of goods	Stable	Subject to changes.

The physical distribution manager should secure as complete information as possible on the market areas to be served, on the level and stability of demand, costs of warehousing, capital required for warehousing and material handling, comparative costs of public and private warehouses. One the basis of data thus collected companies should develop a policy concerning use of solely company owned warehouses (private warehouses) or solely public warehouses (renting or leasing of warehouses) or a combination of the two.

Contract Warehouses

This type of warehousing combines the best characteristics of both public and private warehousing. Contract warehousing dictates a symbiotic long-term relationship with shared risk and lower cost than a public warehouse. Although minimum fixed assets are still required for facilities yet it provides benefits like economies of scale by sharing management, labour, equipment and information resources across a number of clients and above all flexibility and expertise. In short, the contract warehouses can take total responsibility of logistics for a firm, leaving it to develop its expertise in manufacturer in Buffalo USA, uses contracted warehouses. Since 1993, Rich has contract with a contract warehouse company Christial Salvensen, for storage, handling and distribution service at its facilities in New York. Both companies have a symbiotic relationship. Rich does not have to worry about storage space for his products and Christian doesn't have to be concerned with filling space in its warehouses. This leaves recourse/time for Rich to concentrate on expanding distribution network and for Christian to stress upon increasing customer service as well. In many cases, the operating company will have planned the warehouse and commissioned its design and construction and then will arrange for the sale of the warehouse to the financing agency, *e.g.* Food Corporation of India.

On the Basis of Operations

(*a*) Plant or base warehouse (centralised warehouse);

(*b*) Distribution centre warehouse (decentralised warehouse).

Plant or base warehouses are usually company owned warehouses. These are integral part of the plant facilities. Their primary function is to receive products from the end of the assembly line and store them till they are shipped to the distribution centre warehouses.

A distribution centre warehouse is primarily established for movement of goods rather than for storage. It typically serves regional market, consolidates large shipment from different point of production, re-groups products into customer orders.

Other Popular Types of Warehouses

The factors influencing warehousing decision include the types of distribution industry, the firm's strategic goals, financial capacities, product characteristics such as perish ability, size, seasonality, intrinsic value, quantity and potential for obsolescence, strength of the competition and state of the general economy.

Due to the complex nature of the variables influencing the warehousing decision, the companies constantly keep on trying to develop specialised types of storages. Cutting across the above mentioned main forms of warehouses are various specialised warehouse storage types. For most part, these types of storage are determined by the product characteristics. Among possible types of warehouses following are the main ones.

(*i*) ***General Merchandise Warehouses :*** These warehouse account for the largest percentage of all warehousing activities. This type of warehouse can be public or private and many or many not have custom or free-trade-zone facilities. They deal in all commodities except specialized or commodity goods. They tend to be specialized driven by the storage and material handling factors. *e.g.,* warehouse handling commodities like paper, small appliance and household supplies.

(*ii*) ***Refrigerated/Cold storage warehouse :*** Perishable goods need to be kept at certain low temperatures to preserve their quality. The cost of making a cold storage warehouse is comparatively higher than other forms of warehouses (especially so in India) and thus they are generally public in nature. Many firms with ample resources opt for private cold storages. But in other developed and developing countries they are usually contracted in nature. Due to expensive nature of cold storage warehousing, another variation of warehousing has been developed in this category like warehousing for fruits etc. and these they can be stored at a controlled temperature and humidity levels. This can be down with the help of air conditioners etc. and thus the fixed costs are lower.

(*iii*) ***Special commodity warehouses :*** These are warehouses which are specialized to handle particular or bulk commodity *e.g.* wood, agricultural goods, building materials etc. The advantage of this warehouse is the customisation of material handling techniques to those of the product. These can be private or public, centralised or decentralised.

(*iv*) ***In-bound warehouses (shops) :*** The In-bound warehouses are businesses that bring in imported merchandise, store and display the merchandise the tourist shops that sell for export or sell the merchandise which is directly exported. The most common example is an in-bound warehouse (shop) which sells liquor at the airport. Out-bound passengers collect the liquor as they board the out-bound international flights (thus the merchandise is exported).

(*v*) ***Open bounded warehouses :*** Open bounded warehouse are premises where imported goods and materials are processed and manufactured into other products. These new products are then exported or applicable duties are collected.

(*vi*) ***Bounded warehouses :*** Distributors often use a special type of warehouse that enables them to produce, transfer and store products without having to pay excise taxes and duties on them. These are warehouses licensed by the government to various parties. *e.g.* warehouses on the docks.

(*vii*) ***Free-Trade-Zones :*** These are zones where the companies are exempt or have reduced customs duty liability. In free-trade-zone warehouses the companies can store goods, in excess of their requirement, by obtaining a permit.

(*viii*) ***Combination warehouses :*** These are warehouses which aim at providing a combination of all the above facilities.

A company can choose any of the above warehouses to serve its functions. Its operating structure *i.e.,* the functions performed by a warehouse more or less remains the same.

Choosing the right kind of warehouse is not the end of the warehouse management process. One also has to pay attention if internal warehouse management as well.

MULTIMODAL TRANSPORT

Multimodal Transport means transport of cargo from premiers by more than are mode, under a single contact evidence by a single transitions and through freight rate of liability. Thus this is the transport of merchandise using two or more means of transportation from the location designated by the exporter to the location of the importer where the carrier is responsible for taking custody of the merchandise.

Features of Multi-modal Transport System

1. Goods mainly in international trade pass through the hands of more then one carrier and more than one mode of transport.
2. Under Conventional system of sequenced transport, the consignee enters into separate contract with each other.
3. The liability of each carrier is limited to the carrier to the carriage performed by him.
4. The carrier of his agent has to attend to all arrangements required for transshipment of goods from one mode to another, including warehousing.

Advantages of Multi-modal Transport

1. Minimises time loss at transshipment point.
2. Provides faster transit of goods.
3. Reduces burden of documentation and formalities.
4. Saves cost.
5. Establishes only one agency to deal with.

Different Types of Operators

1. Sea/Air

(*i*) There is company of sea transport and speed in air transport.

(*ii*) Mainly for eastern or European routes.

(*iii*) Mainly used for high value goods like electronic, computer and high seasonal goods like fashion wear.

2. Air/Road (Truck)

(*i*) Through road transport is incidental to air transport *i.e.* pick-up delivery.

(*ii*) It is also used across national boundaries to connect with main bases of airport.

3. Rail/Road/Inland waterways—sea-rail/road/inland waterways

Inland mode of transport such as road rail and waterways are used to reach sea ports in the country of origin or from the sea port of the country of destination to inland destination.

4. Mini bridge

(*i*) Two international inter modal options are mini land bridge (mini bridge) and micro bridge.

(*ii*) Mini bridge is a variant of land bridge is which freight movements originates or terminates at a point within the United States.

5. Macro bridge

Terminates at an inland point rather than a port, otherwise it is the same as mini bridge.

6. Land bridge

(*i*) Its rate embrace two maritime tariff and surface transport rate.

(*ii*) Sea-Land-Sea.

7. Micro bridge

Micro bridge return to door-to-door service available along the west coast of the United States rather than traditional part-to-part.

Supplier of Transportation Services

Transportation services are offered by a combination of suppliers historically, government policy limited provides to single-mode operation. This restriction was designed to promote competition between modes and thus limit the potential for monopoly practices experienced in the early rail road ear.

The limitations were lifted following deregulation so that carriers could develop integrated inter modal services to more efficiently and effectively meet the needs of customers.

Following are the example of carriers that are representative of each category.

1. Single-mode Operator : The most basic carrier type is a single-mode operator that offers services utilising only one transport mode. This degree of fours allows a carrier to become highly specialised, competent and efficient.

However, the approach events significant difficulties for inter modal transport become it requires negotiation and a transition with each individual carrier. Airlines are an example of a single mode carrier for both freight and passenger services since they only offer service from airport to airport the shipper or passenger is responsible for movement to and from the airport.

A series of single-mode operation require more management effort and, thus increase cost.

2. Specialised carrier : Over the past several decades a serious problem existed is small-shipment transportation. It was difficult for a common carrier to provide a reasonably priced small-shipment service because of significant overhead cost associated with terminal and line service. This overhead forced motor carriers to assign a minimum charge for handling any shipment. Rail roads do not offer small shipment service. As a result of the minimum charge and the lack of low-cost rail alternatives on opportunity existed for companies offering specialized service to enter the small-shipment or package-service market.

Package services represent an important part of transportation infrastructure, and the influence of carriers in this segment is increasing because of their size and inter modal capabilities.

Basic Package Service

Numerous carriers offer package delivery services within commercial zones of metropolitan areas. This type of service is classified as exempt common carriage. Other carriers offer package delivery service on an intrastate and interstate basis *e.g.* Indian Postal services UPS The original service offered by UPS was contract delivery of local shipments for department stores.

Over the past two decades UPS has made substantial inroads into more diverse intercity package movements.

In fact, UPS has expanded its scope of overall operating authority by shipping packages that conform to specified size and weight restrictions nationwide and globally for consumers and business enterprise.

1. ***Electronic tracking :*** Monitors shipment from pick-up to delivery.
2. ***Advanced label imaging system :*** (AIIS) Bar code package.
3. ***Delivery information service :*** Automatic proof of delivery via bar coding.
4. ***Customer clearance service :*** Expedited service for UPS International Air system for online delivery information.
5. ***Consignee billing :*** Management and direct payment of in-bound customer transportation charges.
6. ***Inventory Express :*** Logistical support (Inventory control, distribution and reporting) for time secretive products requiring for reliable retribution.
7. ***On-call air pick-up :*** Save-day pickup for all UPS air services via customer phone all UPS properties. Facility development for site tearing close to UPS operation.

Quality of service depends on various factors, some of which are as follows:

(*i*) Speed

(*ii*) Door-to-door capability

(*iii*) Reliability

(*iv*) Security
(*v*) Safely
(*vi*) Inedibility
(*vii*) Availability

Ranking of Carrier Selection Determined

1. Transit time reliability or inconsistency
2. Door-to-door transportation rate or cost
3. Total door-to-door transit time
4. Willingness of carrier to negotiate rate charges
5. Financial stability of the carrier
6. Equipment availability
7. Frequency of service
8. Pickup and delivery service
9. Freight loss and damage
10. Shipment expedite
11. Quality of operating personnel
12. Shipment tracing
13. Willingness of carrier to negotiate service changes
14. Scheduling flexibility
15. Line haul services
16. Claim processing
17. Quality of carrier salesmanship
18. Special equipment

Containerisation

The system is a long established one and was carried out in a somewhat primitive form in the North Atlantic Coastal Track in the 1930s, when the vessel were called van ships.

The concept gained momentum in 1955 when an American named Malcolm Mclean devised a new way to ship the goods. Lorry body (Wheels and all) was detached from the drivers cab and lifted on the deck of the ship, thus completely taking away the work of workers to handle the individual items inside the cargo compartment .Mr. Mclean's first ship, an oil tanker called the 'Ideal -X' made its initial voyage from New York to Houston is 1956 with lorry bodies on its deck.

This method soon gave way to the use of metal containers that could be separated from the lorry's chassis and wheels. In 1965 ships with containers onboard (which could be stacked several high aboard the ship) began crossing the Atlantic. The adoption of standard container sizes allowed any box to be transported on any ship.

By 1967 dual purpose ships, carrying loose cargo in the hold and containers on deck were giving way to container only vessels that moved thousands of boxes at a time.

The container crane, made it possible to efficiently load and unload containers. Cost of shipping was reduced since ships could be loaded by a few dozen workers in place of hundreds and also pilferage was much reduced. The need to build wooden crates to protect individual items was made unnecessary.

The holds of container vessels are fitted with a series of angle guides, adequately quality cross braced, to accept the container.

Containerisation is a method of distribution of goods using containers. The use of containers has not only facilitated but has also revolutionised the carriage of goods among developed countries. Exporters in developing countries are also making greater use of containers for the transportation of the goods. The enactment of multi Modal Transportation of goods Act, 1993 has enabled exporters from India to use exporters from India to use containers for transportation of export cargo. Train or road to the seaports carries the containers, where they are loaded on the ships for onward transportation to their destination.[9]

Exporters do not need to carry the cargo to the seaports any longer rather they can approach the container freight station or the inland container depot (ICD) to book the cargo there for transportation to the destination.

The custom clearance of the cargo is provided at ICDs and in the process, the exporters are able to save lot of time. The packing of cargo in a container can be done either in the container depot or in the factory of the exporter.

The holds of container vessels are fitted with a series of angle guides adequately cross braced, to accept the container. Such holds are completely dedicated to either the 20 or 40 ft. container. The containers are stacked such that, they are above rests securely on the weight bearing comes castings of the one below.

The angle guides also facilitate discharging and loading by guiding spreader frankest of container arenas onto the comes castings of container without any need for the crave driver to make any five adjustments to line up the lifting frame.

Container berth are either purpose built for exclusive container use, or multipurpose in which container and other types of cargo vessels are handled. A purpose built container berth is usually the more efficient and produces the most productive container throughput. The most modern one would be computer operated.

Time spent in loading and discharging containers varies by port and circumstances.

In very broad terms one can attain 25/30 containers per hour for discharging cargo whilst fort exports the figure is 20/25 hour per crave of single container capacity.

Leasing of Container

Containers are taken on lease by carriers from container manufacturing companies or leasing companies who own containers. There are four types of leasing arrangements.

1. ***Trip Lease :*** Trip lease or short term lease. The lease is for one voyage or one trip (voyage implies to and fro and trip connotes one leg only.

2. ***Long-term Lease :*** Containers are usually leased for a period of 3 years to 5 years.

3. ***Financial Lease :*** This is more of a hire-purchase or installment purchase rather than a lease as in this case at the end of the term for which containers are taken on financial lease, the ownership of the container is transferred to the lessee.

4. ***Master lease :*** In this case, one ship-owner concludes a deal with a container leasing company for a period of usually 1-2 years whereby he guarantees that a minimum number of containers will always be under his lease from the leasing company. Against this guarantee, the container leasing company also assures the ship owner at the various parts as agreed upon between the two contracting parties.

Lease rent is charged at per day container. The rate depends upon the supply and demand situation. The International container lessons Association has drawn up forms of contract to assist the working of the leasing market. The rent component can also include insurance premium for loss/damage to a limited extent.

Users normally prefer to lease a container than owning it. This is more true of ship-owners who use bulk of the containers available. Owning involves investment of capital, maintenance, workshop management et, but owning containers provide self-reliance to ship-owners and also source of advertisement for their lines wherever containers more.

There is Institute of International Containers Lessors (IICL) New York, which covers the largest nine lessors, of which three largest number control 63 per cent of the leased fleet containers and 27 per cent of the total owned and leased units world wide. (These figures change from time to time). The "Big Nine" are Genstar, Trama Merica, Triton,

Transocean, LEA, Tax tainer (U.S.A.). Tip hook, sea containers (U.K.) and Clou (Germany).

INLAND CONTAINER DEPOT

The concept of ocean-going containers was introduced in India for the first time in 1968 is a seminar held jointly by the Indian National Ship-owners Association (INSA), Directorate General of Shipping, the Shipping Corporation of India. (SCI) and the All Indian Shippers Council (AISC) at Mumbai.

In early 19703, the SCI acquired the first semi-container ship with three holds designed to carry containers along with two holds full general cargo other shipping companies like India steam Navigation Co-Ltd. and India Steam Navigation Co-Ltd. followed on the steps of the SCI. India steamship company went ahead to acquire a small cellular container ship.

In 1971 Cochin Port received containers for the first time from a conventional general cargo vessel of the American President Lines. They were handled by the ship's.

In 1973, the American President lines began scheduling their cellular feeder container ships to Mumbai and brought the necessary. Handling equipment with then. The action was repeated by the lines of European and other countries who also thereafter started scheduling their cellular ships to Indian Part.

However, India began to seriously adopt containerisation only in 1978. Major parts like Mumbai, Cochin, Chennai, Haldia/Kolkatta commenced to equip themselves for handling container ships and containers in the appropriate way.

Shippers and consignees also responded to the opportunities and benefits in containerisation. The buyers of Indian goods abroad stipulated in their letters of credit that the goods should be containerised. Hence, despite the need for heavy investments and numbers problems in smooth flow of good, India was forced into containerisation to stay with the dominant trend is the world economy.

INLAND CONTAINER DEPOT (ICD)—ROLES AND FUNCTIONS

The full benefits of containerisation can be obtained only if the containers are used to move to the location of the original cargo generation point. The Government of India decided to set up inland container depots (ICDs) which are also called dry parts. Shipping formalities can be completed in ICDs for containerised cargoes instead of at the exit gateways port.

Inland container depots are interfaces between connecting modes of transportation. In Inland container depot is an organisation offering a total package of activities to handle and control container and general cargo flows between road, rail and waterways, and vice versa, resulting in maximum service for inland transportation at minimum cost.

Normally ICDs provide the following service.

1. ***Handling of Containers :*** Handling of containers from road, rail and barges to a temporary storage area container.
2. ***Intermediate Storage :*** Intermediate between the various transportation modes. Special containers and or cargo may require additional provision such as refrigeration services and special areas for dangerous cargo.
3. ***Receipt and Delivery of Containers and General Cargo :*** This may include activates such as weighting inspection of seals and damages, sticker and safety plate control and container information control. Stuffed containers may be received from the satellite container freight stations (CFS) in ready condition to be transported to the exit port. Shippers may also directly bring. Less than container load (LCL) cargoes for the purpose of consolidation and dispatch.
4. ***Cargo Consolidation and Distribution :*** If the container cannot be received or delivered directly at

the final consignee's door. In this case, containers are stuffed with or destuffed for LCL. Depending upon the direction of the cargo movement prior to dispatch.

5. ***Depot Functions for the Storage of Empty Containers*** : Space may also be required for temporary storage of loaded containers awaiting movement out of ICD.
6. ***Other facilities*** : Include container cleaning services, pre trip traits of reefer containers to check the function of refrigeration equipment, maintenance and repair services for container, container handling equipment, refrigeration equipment, road chassis etc. In this respect, ICD should make itself a self sufficient unit.
7. ***Custom's Clearance Activities:*** At inland terminals could help to decrees the dwell time of containers in deep-sea ports. These activities include checking of LCL cargo prior to stuffing or after stripping, checking container seals, assessment and valuation of cargoes, perusal of container manifests, and soon. The transport of containers under bond to ICDs from deep sea ports is a necessary feature of well-developed multi-modal transport systems because this has proved to be a time and cost saving function.
8. **Physical Distribution Service** : These can be provided economically at or close to the ICDs. Garments can be ironed and packed, prices tagged on consumer goods, liquids in bulk can be butted in short, a variety of cargo related services to finished goods can be placed near the ICD itself. For agricultural products, ICDs may provide refrigeration plants and warehousing facilities to prepare meat fish and vegetables for export.

Indian ICDs performs many of the possible functions outlined above. These include stuffing, destuffing, locking, sealing, providing trains chassis, railway floats repairs, handling equipment storage facilities for reefer, customers examination and processing of customer documents, issuance of combined transport documents by carriers.

ICD is a declared customers Area for the purpose of import and export but only limited facilities of noting of shipping bills, valuation and examination of export cargo are afforded at ICD exports however are deemed to be effected from the gateway export only.

ICDs are connected with gateway parts. Within 24 hours of landing, the containers coassignee to the ICDs are dispatched by rail. At the parts, ICDs containers and transshipment containers are moved on probity basis similarly, stuffed containers, on completion of customer's formalities at the ICD, are dispatched to the terminal part writhing 24 hours. The railways provide the transport link between the ICDs and the gateway ports.

CONTAINER FREIGHT STATIONS (CFS)

CFS have been established to speed up export cargo can to specially help small exporters whose consignments are less than container (LCL) loads. The CFS has facilities of modern go down accommodation under export supervision. Facilities of banking, custom examination, clearance, safe handling, stuffing, sealing and transportation of containers are available. Both import and export consignment are handled here.

Location of ICDs and CFSs is regulated by the ministry of commerce of the Government of India. While this ministry is encouraging liberalisation and competitiveness with a view to making transport more attractive and customer friendly.

The supportive network of surface transport with the location of container freight station and Inland container depots has to be in the hinterland. The location depends upon the potentiality of generating volume of export cargo or where distribution of imports cargoes can be easily facilitated.

CFSs and ICDs are complementary to each other CFSs are cargo aggregating points, which should conveniently feed the ICDs for carriage to gateway parts in sizable quantities and over long distances may be brought over the same route to an ICD for distributing to the various users.

ESTABLISHMENT AND OPERATION OF ICDs UNDER CONCOR

As the country heads towards achieving containerisation in greater proportions the development of inland container depot (ICDs) and container freight stations (CFSs) becomes crucial. Contrassy to its dubious status as being a laggard in containerisation, the country is making serious efforts to container corporation of India (CONCOR), which has taken up the formidable task of setting up ICDs and CFSs spanning the length and breadth of India.

The Indian Railways set up seven ICDs, the first being at Guntur in December 1980, followed by Bangalore in 1981. The need was however felt to set up a separate undertaking under the Railways to manage the ICDs and CFSs. Hence CONCOR was established in 1988 to provide for an integrated development of ICDs and CFSs to meet future growth requirements.

EXPORT CLEARANCE AT ICDs

The exporter should mention the name of name of 'Port of Exit' and serial number of containers. The exporter should obtain in advance space availability certificate from the Railway combined Terminal operator.

1. ***Checking Details of the Shipping Bill :*** The shipping bill should mention details of goods, their classification name of the port of exit, identification mark, number of containers, weight and value of goods. Contents of cargo should be declared and proper statistical code number be given. GR forms should accompany, without fail, the shipping bills.

2. ***Scrutiny of Shipping Bills :*** Duly completed shipping bills are put in the Noting Box provided at the ICD. The receiving clerk after noting these scrutinises and accompanying documents. The receiving clerk will give a running serial number as shipping bill no discrepancy is found. Otherwise, these may be returned for resubmission after correction.

3. ***Classification and Assessment :*** The central Registration unit of the ICD completes the classification and assessment. The rate of duty is filled by appraisement department. The original shipping bill is retained and the balance six copies are handed over to exporter for completion of examination.

4. ***GR Formalities :*** A full set of GR forms has to be submitted along with the shipping bills. The full value of export will be verified on the GR form.

The assuring officer will retain the original GR form for release to the RBR. Duplicate copies are retained at ICD. Shipment certificate on the GR form shall be furnished after customs examination of the export cargo and sealing of container by proper officer at ICD. Duplicate copies are then released to the exporter for his use.

5. ***Examination of Goods :*** Custom Inspector/examiner conducts the examination of goods, heaping in view the restrictions under Acts, Rates and Regulations. After examination, goods are shifted into the container and same are sealed by the customs officers. The custom officer records on the shipping bill—

1 Quality of goods loaded;

2. No of packages shut out.

The exporter at this stage is to prepare and present as invoice and container-wise packing list (both in four copies) indicating—

(*i*) Number of packages with marks and numbers;

(*ii*) Description and total quantity net weight packed in each container. The Appraiser/Superintendent/ Examiner with the details present these two documents for certification;

(*iii*) Duplicate copy of the shipping bill is retained at the ICD and exchange control copy is returned to exporter.

6. *Transit to Gateway Port/Port of Exit :* The two transfer copies are sealed in an envelope for custody of the Railways who are responsible for subsequent presentation to the custom officer at the Gateway Port-Exit Port.

7. *Procedure to be followed at Exit Port :* The sealed containers are allowed to be exported in preventive supervision on verification with the seal being intact, without any further examination. However, if seal is found tampered with, examination may be done at the Port.

1. The custom officer at the port will be entitled to open and examine the contents of any container.
2. The preventive officer at the port will endorse the two transference copies of the shipping bills regarding the containers being intact and custom seal being intact, and adds his dated signature.
3. The steamer agent shall be required to file the export manifest in duplicate regarding cargo containers with the container unit of export department of the customs house.
4. After that shipment transference copies of the shipping bills shall be sent to ICD within 48 hours of shipment.

8. *Endorsement of Shipment :* From Gateway Port on quick drawback payment section copy of shipping bills.

The exporter, after enquiring from the export unit of ICD regarding receipt of transference copies shall obtain certificate to this effect on the quick drawback copy of the shipping bill and can claim drawback from Quick Drawback Payment Section.

AT THE ICD

1. On arrival of the containers at the ICD, the Railway Road Carriers will present the sealed cover to the Customs Officer. The particulars of the containers, seals etc. Shall be checked with reference to the transshipment permit received followed by the endorsement of the transshipment permit.
2. On de-stuffing of the container at the ICD, which is carried out in the presence of the Customs Officer, a representative of the Railways or Road Carriers, the packages should be tallied with the documents and marks and numbers compared with reference to the manifest.
3. The clearance of the goods for home consumption from ICD will be on the basis of Bills of Entry to be filed by the Importer at the ICD.
4. The B/E's details is noted against the copy of the submanifest followed by the duty assessment procedure involving classification, assessment, payment of duty and examination.

Table 4.2. Dimensions of Container

Overall Dimensions	Inside Dimensions	Dorr Dimen-sions	Cubic Capant m^3	Tare wt. kg. (men)	Gross wt. (men)
$20 \times 8 \times 8^1/_2$ (6.1 × 2-4 × 2.6)	5-98 × 2-345 × 2.400	2.355 × 2.290	32.7	2450	24000
$40 \times 8 \times 8^1/_2$	12.0/5 × 2.345 × 2.345 × 2-362	2.335 × 2-260	66.3	3700	30480

BY USE

Containers can also be classified by their uses.

(*a*) ***General Purpose Containers :*** This type of containers are closed and are suitable for the carriage of all types of general cargo and with suitable temporary modification for the carriage of bulk cargoes, both solid and liquid. Containers are basically a steel framework with steel glass reinforced plastic or aluminum alloy used for pudding. the floors are either hardwood timber planted or plywood sheeted. Access for loading and unloading is through full width floors. Cargo securing/lashing points are located at floor level at the base of the side walls.

(*b*) ***Insulated containers :*** Protect against head loss or gain and are used in conjunction with a blown-air-refrigeration system to convey Perishable or other cargo which needs to be carried under temperature contract.

(*c*) ***Fruit containers :*** Insulated container with internal dimensions slightly longer.

(*d*) ***Refrigerated containers :*** Are fitted with their own refrigeration units which require an electrical supply for their operation.

(*e*) ***Bulk containers :*** Are designed for the carriage of dry powders and gramlar substances in bulk. To facilitate top loading three circular hatches (500 mm. dia) are fitted in same containers of the roof structure. For discharge a hatch is fitted in the right hand door of the container.

(*f*) ***Ventilated containers :*** Are of steel construction and have full length ventilation galleries sited along the top and bottom side rails, allowing passive ventilation of the cargo. Ingress of water is prevented.

(*g*) ***Flat rack containers :*** Are ideal for uncontainer-able cargo.

(*h*) ***Open top containers :*** Have top loading facility suitable were height of cargo is in excess of the height of the standard general purpose container.

(*i*) ***Half-height version :*** Of the open top container is designed for the carriage of heavy dense cargoes such as steel, pipes and tubes etc.

(*j*) ***Tank containers :*** Generally contracted with the carriage of a specific product or range of products in mind.

(*k*) *Open sided containers* : Accommodate specific commodities such as plywood, perishable commodities and livestock.

(*l*) *Hanger containers* : Are used for dry cargo and are equipped with removable beams in the upper part. They are used for the shipment of garments on hangers.

(*m*) *Bin containers* : Have no doors, ideal for heavy douse cargoes such as steel pipes.

Average operational life of a container is 12 years.

Advantages of Containerisation

(*i*) Permits a door to door service which may be from factory production side to retail distributing store an overall distance of may be 1000 cm.

(*ii*) No intermediate handling at terminal (part) transshipment points.

(*iii*) The absence of intermediate handling plus quick transit permits less risk of cargo damage and pilferage.

(*iv*) Low risk of cargo damage and pilferage enables more favourable cargo premiums to be obtained compared with conventional cargo shipments.

(*v*) Elimination of intermediate handling at terminal transfer points *i.e.* parts, enables substantial labour savings to be realised.

(*vi*) Less packing needs for containerised shipments.

(*vii*) Cargo arrives in better condition.

(*viii*) Rates are likely to remain more competitive when compared with conventional tonnage.

(*ix*) Transits are much quicker: Combination of faster vessels the rationalisation of parts of call and substantially quicker cargo handling.

(*x*) Encourages trade development and quicker payment of export invoices.

(*xi*) Permitted fleet rationalisation.

(*xii*) Faster transits encouraging many importance to hold reduced stocks spares.

(*xiii*) Container vessels attain much improved utilisation and are generally more productive.

(*xiv*) Stimulating trade expansion through much improved service standards.

(*xv*) Provision of through documentation.

(*xvi*) Provision of through rate.

(*xvii*) More reliable transits.

(*xviii*) Emergency of new markets.

(*xix*) Overall total quality service.

Manufacture of Containers with Specific Reference to India

Containers are manufactured by many international companies and they are leased to shipping companies/users. Far east now plays a vital role in container manufacture, with 90 per cent of world capacity and about 80 per cent of actual container production being located in South Korea, Taiwan, China, Thailand and Indonesia. The International containers Manufacturers Association covers over two thirds of the annual world container production and is towards global membership base. Its headquarters are situated at Hong Kong. India, which has been manufacturing containers to a limited extent, with proper encouragement and development can become leading base. Transport containers originally started by Nathani steels of Mumbai, now belong to Dalmia Mittal Group. They have been expanding their production capacity. The company has also set-up a reefer container unit in collaboration with Morteo Industries of Italy. This plant is located near Patalganga about 70 kilometres south of Mumbai and has capacity to produce 20 feet, 40 feet and 48 feet containers.

Varun Sea Ltd promoted by V.B. Patel Group has a 100 per cent export-oriented unit to manufacture dry freight marine containers and marine freight refrigerated containers. The plant is located at Bhumel village near Nadiad. The needed technical know-how and engineering services are procured through a tie-up with Container Engineering International (CEI) which is a wholly owned subsidiary of Braf Gusbi of Germany.

Feddrs Lloyd group and Italy's Cobra Spa have a joint venture to manufacture. 20 feet refrigerated containers, targeted at the processed food sector. The plant is located at Kandla in Gujarat.

Important Features of Shipping Containers

1. Manufactured to the 'International Standards Organisation' (ISO) specification in respect to their dimensions

2. They are made of

(*i*) Some are made of aluminium and steel, they are now mostly made. entirely of a special steel called 'cortern' which is a rust prohibitive type of steel.

(*ii*) Steel frame, fitted with 8 weight bearing corner casting fitted into the 8 corners.

(*iii*) Filled in with corrugated steel panels which are between 1-5 mm to 3.00 mm thick. Normally 4 locking bass which interlock with the frame top and bottom.

(*iv*) 27 mm thick wooden ply floor.

(*v*) Supported on load bearing cross bearers approx 12" apart, making the container capable of withstanding loads of 20 to 35 tons.

3. They are heavy by 2-5 ton for 20' and 4 tons 40'.

4. Designed to be fully waterproof including the doors which are fitted with full wrap around seals

5. When badmouthed through the available holes in the door gear they are fairly secure but can be made more secure

by the fitting of a lock box which conceals the lock from interference.

6. Container is sold by shipping lines after 10 years of age.
7. (*i*) They have variety of columns

   (*ii*) The type of point is usually chlorinated rubber or vinyl both manufactured to resists sea water, sun and abrasion.
8. (*i*) A container exposed to sunlight and cold can cause condensation, especially if the interior of the contents are damp.

   (*ii*) Condensation can normally be easily prevented by the use of disposable dehumifigation.

Stuffing of Cargo in a Container

Stuffing of cargo in a container is concerned with packing of the cargo. The exporter or the shipper should formulate a proper storage plan prior to packing a container. This would help the shipper to.

(*i*) Achieve optimal utilisation of container capacity.

(*ii*) Simplify and increase the speed of packing and unpacking.

(*iii*) Plan for necessary cargo searing aids well is advance.

The exporter should have the following information for the storage planning.

1. The type of container suitable for the cargo.
2. The exact weight and measurement of the cargo to be loaded and its packaging.
3. Exact inside dimension and permissible load limits of the containers.

The plan for packing should be developed on the basis of the factors outlined above as this will decide the kind of packing the exporter should use. The following rules should be followed, while packing the cargo.

1. The different types of packages (for example card board boxes and wooden boxes).

2. The container should be lined with paper or foil in the case of specially sometime goods.

3. The container should be made odourless or property washed out in case the good are sensitive to odour .

4. The packing in the boxes should be carefully checked before stuffing them into container.

5. The exporter should not pack together.

(*i*) The wet goods with dry goods.

(*ii*) Goods with protruding parts, sharp edges or corners with goods in comparatively soft packing such as ... or card board boxes.

(*iii*) Dusty goods with dust sensitive goods.

(*iv*) By placing the heavy packets on light packets.

(*v*) Odour emitting goods with odour sensitive goods.

Precautions for Packing the Container

The exporter should take the following precautions while sending the goods through container.

The container should be thoroughly got checked to ensure that—

1. There are so holes or cracks in the walls and roofs.
2. Its doors can be easily operated.
3. Locking doors and handles function properly
4. There are no placards/labels pasted of the previous cargo.
5. Container is waterproof.
6. Container is dry from inside.
7. Container is clean free of dust and cargo residue.

8. Container should be odourless in the case of odour sensitive goods.

Checking of Container After Packing

The exporter should catch the container once the cargo has been stuffed into it to ensure the following:

1. A copy of the packing list is fixed at one easily visible position inside the container.
2. Door handles are seared by seals to reduce the risk of pilferage.
3. In case of open top container, it should be ensured that the tarpaulins and the ropes are correctly fixed.

Arrangement of Container

The exporter should approach the cargo agent for hiring the container. "The cargo can be sent on FCL/LCL basis. FCL stand for Full Container Load and LCL stands for Less than container load. The exporter can arrange for packing of the cargo in the confiner is his factory if so desired. The cargo's agent will arrange for the packing and thereafter the containers are shifted to the container depot. Alternatively, the exporter can bring the cargo to the container depot and the cargo is stuffed in the container after custom clearance. The government has established number of inland container depots to provide the facility of export through containers by sea routes. The containers after custom clearance are moved to the sea port for their loading on their way to destination. The movement of the containers can be done either by road or by rail.

Container Marking

For identification, containers have marking, showing:

1. Owner code, serial number and check digit;
2. Country code and type code;
3. Maximum cross and tare weight.

REFERENCES

1. *Logistics Management*, Reji Ismail, II Edition, Excel Books New Delhi, 2005.
2. *Text Book of Logistics and Supply Chain Management* by DK Agrawal—Macmillan Publication, New Delhi, 2005, pp. 9-16.
3. *Text Book of Logistics and Supply Chain Management* by DK Agrawal—Macmillan Publication New Delhi, 2005, pp. 45-67.
4. *Logistics Management—Supply Chain Imperative* by Vinod Sople, Pearson Education Publication, New Delhi, 2005.
5. *Logistics Management—Supply Chain Imperative* by Vinod Sople, Pearson Education Publication, New Delhi, 2005.
6. *Containerisation, Multimodal Transport and Infrastructure Development in India* by Dr. K.V. Hariharan, Shroff Publication, New Delhi, 2005.
7. *Survey of Indian Industry 2005—The Annual Hindu Publication*, The Hindu Group Publication, Chennai, 2005.
8. *Manual—Institute of Rail Transport on Multi-modal Transport and Containerisation*, New Delhi, 2004.
9. *Hand Book on Multi-modal Transport (Containerisation) and Logistics Management of Institute of Rail Transport,* New Delhi 2005.
10. *Logistics Management* by Reji Ismail-Excel Books. New Delhi, 2005, p. 125.

Container Corporation of India and Its Practices

Chapter 5

Container Corporation of India Ltd. (CONCOR), is now an undisputed market leader having the largest network of 58 ICDs/CFSs in India. In addition to providing inland transport by rail for containers, it has also expanded to cover management of Ports, air cargo complexes and establishing cold-chain. It has and will continue to play the role of promoting containerisation of India by virtue of its modern rail wagon fleet, customer friendly commercial practices and extensively used Information Technology. The company developed multimodal logistics support for India's International and Domestic containerisation and trade. Though rail is the main stay of our transportation plan, road services and also provided to cater to the need of door-to-door services, whether in the International or Domestic business.[1]

STRATEGIC INTENTS

Mission : To join with community partners and stake holders to make concor a company of outstanding quality by providing responsive, cost effective, efficient and reliable logistics solutions to customers through synergy with community partners and ensuring profitability and growth.[2]

Objectives

- A customer focussed, performance driven, result-oriented organisation, focussed on providing value for money to our customers.
- To maximise productive utilisation of resources, deliver high quality of services, and be recognised as setting the standards for excellence.
- Look for new and better ways to provide innovative services. Will aim for customer convenience and satisfaction, learn from our competitors and always strive for excellence.
- Set measurable performance goals to support the objectives and mission of organisation and work as a professional, competent and dedicated team for the organisation to achieve excellence in all areas of our business and operations by benchmarking ourselves with our competitors.
- Will follow highest standards of business ethics and add social value for the community at large by discharging social obligations as a responsible corporate entity.
- Will maintain absolute integrity, honesty, transparency and fair-play in all our official dealings and strive to maintain high standards of morality in our personal life.

CONCOR's strategic position in the logistics market is characterised by:

- Relatively monopolistic market position as a sole-provider of rail-hauls for containers;
- Strong relationship with Indian Railways coupled with an MoU for providing for guaranteed transits on 'liner corridors';
- network of terminals across the country, which captures traffic at the production/consumption centers;

Though rail is the mainstay of CONCOR transportation plan, road services are also being provided to meet market demand. The company also operates container terminals across the country to both external trade and domestic businesses, requiring inland freight movement by rail. CONCOR's core business is characterised by three distinct activities, that of a carrier, a terminal operator, and a warehouse operator.

CARRIER

Rail is the mainstay of CONCOR's transportation plans and strategy. Majority of CONCOR terminals are rail-linked, with rail as the main carrier for haulage. Facilities are, however, provided for first and last mile transportation by road also. CONCOR benefits from a close relationship with the Indian Railways. Several of its terminals are situated on leased Railway-land. Many of its key operating personnel are on secondment from Indian Railways or have previously been employed by the Indian Railways. Wagons and operational support from Indian Railways have always been available to the company. As rail is price-competitive over long distances, the price advantage can be passed on to clients, thus allowing for flexible and competitive pricing. The rail link also plays a major role in decongesting our ports and the road corridors that lead to these ports. Though rail is the mainstay of CONCOR's transportation plan, some CONCOR terminals are exclusively road-fed as well. We provide 94 per cent of our inland transport through the Indian Railways network. Road services are mostly in the form of supplementary services to provide the door to door linkages having carried the bulk of long lead by rail. However, whereever it is operationally or economically a superior option, road is used as an alternative to rail as well.

TERMINAL AND CFS OPERATOR

CONCOR started operations in November 1989 with 7 Inland Container Depots (ICDs). We have since extended the network to a total of 58 terminals, of which 48 are export-import container depots, and 9 exclusive domestic container depots. As many as 31 terminals perform the combined role of domestic as well as international terminals. The company expects the number of terminals to increase to 60 in the next few years.

CONCOR's customs bonded Inland Container depots are dry ports in the hinterland, and serve the purpose of bringing all port facilities including Customs clearance to the customer's doorstep. The terminals are almost always linked by rail to the Indian Railway network, unless their size or location dictates that they be linked by road. The rail links enable us to facilitate the moving of large volumes over long distances in the most cost effective manner. CONCOR's terminals provide a spectrum of facilities in terms of warehousing, container parking, repair facilities, and even office complexes. As CFS operator, CONCOR adds value to the logistics chain by offering value added services such as:

1. Transit warehousing for import and export cargo.
2. Bonded warehousing, *enabling* importers to store cargo and *take partial deliveries,* thereby deferring duty payment.
3. Less than Container Load (LCL) consolidation, and reworking of LCL cargo at nominated *hubs.*
4. Air cargo clearance using bonded trucking.

On the area of domestic business door pick up and door delivery services are the most popular. It also use their terminal network to plan hub and spoke movements that allow single customers to move cargo to multiple locations at a single time, with CONCOR taking care of the distribution and re-distribution requirements.

The key value it offer is the provision of a single-window facility co-ordinating with all the different agencies and services involved in the containerised cargo trade, from Customs, Gateway Ports, and Railways, to road hauliers, consolidators, forwarders, Custom House Agents and shipping lines. To achieve a high degree of customisation, we offer packages designed to provide the most cost-effective combination of road and rail. This enables us to offer services which can be individually tailored to every customers specifications, *minimising customers own efforts.*

HANDLING EQUIPMENT

CONCOR has generally followed a policy of organising specialised cargo/container handling services by deployment of state-of-the-art equipment on contractual basis. In addition, at ICD Tughlakabad, in Delhi, which is the company's flagship terminal, we also own, operate and maintain the most modern and sophisticated handling equipments such as a Rail Mounted Gantry (RMG) , Rubber Tyre Gantries (RTGs), and loaded and empty handling Reach Stackers.

Wagons

After starting operations with make-shift container wagons that were provided by the Indian Railways, CONCOR started acquiring state-of-the-art high speed container flats (BLC wagons), capable of running at 100 kmph. Since last 9 years. These have been progressively introduced on major container circuits in the last three years, as a result of which transit times have reduced and service quality has shown considerable improvement. 7200 such wagons are already deployed, and CONCOR plans to add to that fleet every year to cater to the growth in business as well as to replace outworn rolling stock. CONCOR has also purchased some 7200 container flat wagons from the Indian Railways, which have been since upgraded and retrofitted to also provide improved service quality and better transit times.

INFOTECH

IT forms the backbone of any service industry, where information correlates directly with improved levels of efficiency. In the transport sector, antiquated, cumbersome paper-based procedures cause an enormous waste of time and money. All too often, goods move through transport systems at a frustratingly slow speed, especially in developing countries. The physical side of trade transactions should aspire to become as efficient as the electronic transfer of money. This can be done through working partnerships among all those involved to improve logistics services through the use of information and network technology. A primary component of CONCOR's overall business strategy has been the development of an advanced information system. A container and cargo logistics information system went online at Company's Inland Container Depot at Tughlakabad in 1994 and most other facilities have been equipped with computer systems to monitor traffic movement and maintain inventory records.

CONCOR is using various online applications like Export/ Import Terminal Management System (ETMS), Domestic Terminal Management System (DTMS), Oracle Financials—ERP, HR-Payroll system etc. which are based on Centralised architecture deployed through Citrix environment and running over VSAT-based hybrid network.[3]

RDT's are being used in the ICD/TKD yard and ICD/ Dadri for online container tracking and entry of unloading / loading of containers on to wagons. Interface software was developed for automatic updation of entries through RDT's into CCLS and ETMS database for EXIM operations. RDT's are also interfaced with our Domestic Terminal Management System (DTMS) at DCT/Okhla, TNPM/Chennai and WFD/ Bangalore. This has enabled any user to query the system either through LAN or Web to get the latest status and location of a container in the yard.

Facility for electronic filing (e-filing) of commercial documents of CCLS (Container and Cargo Logistic System) has been provided to customers. This facility enables customers like Shipping lines, Importers, Exporters and

CHA's to file the required documents online for process and take necessary print-outs of processed output through web from anywhere without physically coming to ICD at Tughlakabad. Digital Signatures have been integrated with e-filing on CCLS to make the system more secure.

CONCOR has its own WebServer for providing web interface to the commercial applications *i.e.* ETMS, CCLS, DTMS etc. The web interface enables our customers to access information regarding their shipments by means of the website.

An integrated track and trace system was also implemented on CONCOR website for providing Container Tracking Details, Train Summaries and current train running position.

Fig . 5.1. Organisation Structure of Concor

From the above given organisation structure ,it is evident that Chairman is the topmost authority in CONCOR organisational structure. The next authority is Managing Director which is to be reported by the functional authority like director international marketing operations, director project, director finance, director domestic. Under director International marketing and operations, the reporting authority is international marketing, commercial operations who looks after the international marketing operations.

Under Director Project, the reporting authority is projecting technical and management information system which is responsible for the implementation of Information

Technology implementation. For the financial matters authorities working under Director Finance, finance, accounts, internal audit, Human Resource is also part of it.

The domestic Marketing Director is reported by the authority domestic marketing, communication and communication terminals.

CONCOR ACTIVITIES

CONCOR makes regular marketing efforts to improve business processed to provide for improved quality of customer satisfaction. Some of the practices adopted by the organisation for achieving these goals are listed below:

- On line Information and Container Tracking
- Container Repair and Cleaning Facilities
- Cargo Palletisation, Strapping etc
- Cargo Lashing/Choking Facility
- Fumigation of Cargo/Containers
- Door Delivery/Pick-up of Containerised Cargo
- Container/Cargo Survey
- Pre Deposit Accounts
- Round the Clock Security at Terminals
- Facilitation of Customs Clearance
- Flexible Payment Arrangements

We conduct Customer Satisfaction Survey regularly to get a feedback from the customers and also take action to rectify/improve our services.

CONCOR had also introduced on Company's website "Feedback.com" wherein Customers can obtain information and seek remedies on our services in the format available under menu "Customer Feedback Facility". Prompt action on these observations/suggestions is taken to improve the quality of our services to the customer.[4]

The container traffic in India has grown at a CAGR of 15 per cent since 1991, 2.5 times the average GDP in the same period. With the growth of external trade being faster than GDP, the similar trends are expected to continue in future as well. Similarly the possibilities of growth in container traffic in the domestic sector are immense with continued strong trends in growth of GDP and the need of the industry for value-added services. Logistics ports, large cargo hubs will be the requirement of the industry in very near future, as large retail chains generate the demand for professional managed cargo delivery systems. There will be a need for CONCOR to adopt different strategies for growth in the changed external business environment due to opening up of Rail sector for container train operation for 15 other players. More emphasis will be required on providing total logistics and transport solutions to its customers by seeing the possibilities of expanding the presence of the company in all the segments of the transport value chain in the Exim as well as Domestic segment. Possibilities are to be explored for strategic alliances, both for optimal utilisation of infrastructure as well as expansion into other segments of the value chain.

The emergence of number of new ports *viz.* Mundra, Pipavav, Vizag, Tuticorin, Vallarpadam, Ennore and some minor ports in Gujarat like Porbandar, Okha, Maroli etc. will have a large effect on the hinterland movement of containers in the country. Further, the hinterland penetration levels of the container traffic, which are very low at present, are also bound to see a many-fold increase. This change in the environment offers immense potential for CONCOR to identify new business opportunities and remain the market leader by expanding into new corridors.

Rail remains the main stay of CONCOR's transportation plans, currently. Business trends are now changing towards more and more door-to-door clearances. This needs to provide single window clearance facilities to its customers. This will require close co-ordination and/or alliances with other relevant agencies and transport intermediaries for door-to-door movement of cargo in containers. In order to compete with road sector that provides door-to-door movement of containers on the basis of single price, single window service through a a single document, will be a key USP for the future. The company will continue to adopt cost effective key processes across various terminals and areas of business associated with key critical success factors, the factors which are important to its customers, through the process of Benchmarking. CONCOR has introduced movement of Double Stack Container Trains between Kanakpura (Jaipur) and Pipavav and Kankakpura and Mundra. These trains will provide cost-effective transportation between these ports and ICDs in Northern India.

Due to the presence of Electric wires and other fixed structures on P-way, double stack trains cannot be run elsewhere. CONCOR has also drawn MoUs with some of the leading players in the container transport field for transporting their containers between ports and ICDs.

CONCOR has created a special division to look after the Air Cargo business which has two components (1) Bonded Trucking Services and (2) Air Cargo Complexes. Company arranges bonded trucking services between its ICD's and major international airports like Mumbai, Bangalore, Hyderabad, Amritsar, Chennai and Delhi. Company is expanding these services to/from other locations. Air Cargo Complex at HAL, Bangalore Airport offers all cargo-related services. The other Air Cargo Complexes at Ozar airport, Nasik has commenced operations. Plans are also being worked out for other airports. CONCOR has joint venture with MSIL and HAL in Air Cargo Complexes.

The Joint Venture with M/s. MAERSK A/S *Copenhagen* for third birth at JN Port has placed CONCOR in the category of Port terminal operators. CONCOR has also entered in a JV with Dubai Port World for setting up and managing container terminal at Cochin Port. This has opened new possibilities for further expansion in this field.

For domestic business, CONCOR is committed to bring back to rail a significant share of container stable general goods cargo through aggressive marketing efforts. The main competition in this area comes from road transportation of goods by trucks. However, since we provide better risk coverage, in addition to controlled transit times and overall reliability, we feel we geared to woo traffic that presently uses road. Domestic business has a very large potential for growth today. Given that consumption centers are vast distances away from production points, there will always be a big demand for transport. The setting up of high capacity consumer goods industries also indicates that the growth of non-bulk traffic is expected to be faster than that of bulk traffic, with the shares of both becoming decidedly better than the current 35-65 ratio. Significantly most of this non-bulk traffic is container stable, and represents a huge market potential for CONCOR in the domestic sector.

The main strategy to capture domestic traffic so far has been to run regular scheduled point-to-point services by rail. These CONTRACK services will be expanded to several more origin-destination (O-D) points. Greater efficiency will be introduced through the use of newly acquired rolling stock. Special cargo and corporate will get particular focus by customisation of services, and a wider terminal network will be put in place.

A major aspect of the growth strategy for both international and domestic business will involve the employment of the 'hub and spoke' system to serve the customer completely at his doorstep, while optimising the internal logistics chains within the organisation. In the effort to move from being a service integrator, CONCOR will move towards becoming a Third Party Logistics(3PL) service provider by expanding the core business into areas such as warehousing, refrigerated cargo storage and movement, and the provision of a large number of other value-added services.

As part of the overall strategy to increase market share, CONCOR will also look to provide multi-modal, transportation and logistics consultancy services to its potential users. These could be shippers directly, or intermediate agencies such as shipping lines, forwarding agents, terminal operators etc. Even government bodies and private trade associations chamber of commerce etc. may be targeted as potential clients.

PHYSICAL PERFORMANCE

Physical performance means the no. of containers handled by CONCOR in the last 10 years. These figures are of international and domestic containers handled through ICDs and CFS.Physical figures of CONCOR for the last ten years are displayed as under. As can be seen, the physical performance during the last decade clearly brings out to success story of CONCOR's growth.

Table 5.1 Overall Container Traffic Handled by CONCOR[5]

No.	Year	International	Domestic	Total
1.	1996-97	424741	278801	703542
2.	1997-98	491481	230238	721719
3.	1998-99	576790	225156	801946
4.	1999 -00	664490	238661	903151
5.	2000-01	753368	291360	1044728
6.	2001-02	905058	326775	1231833
7.	2002-03	1031925	351238	1383163
8.	2003-04	1251618	350501	1602119
9.	2004-05	1376516	351460	1727976
10.	2005-06	1556714	373848	1930562
11.	2006-07	1715661	389605	2105266

Interpretation

On the basis of figures from 1996-1997 the container traffic handled by CONCOR was 703542 in which domestic and international containers handled were 2,78,801 and 4,24,741 restively. In ten years of period it increased to 21,05,266, where international containers figures ware 17,15,661 and domestic container. 3,89,605. In ten years period, the rise in international containers was approximately four times where total traffic increased thrice. The figures of domestic traffic also increased, but its shave was limited to 3,89,605.

Cargo Handled Region wise

Table 5.2(*a*). Container Handled in Western Region

Sl.No.	Year	International	Domestic	Total
1.	1996-97	111052	99334	210386
2.	1997-98	126937	40385	167322
3.	1998-99	188038	47454	235492
4.	1999-00	199241	46685	245926
5.	2000-01	222395	45658	268053
6.	2000-02	186646	17515	204161
7.	2002-03	216808	18865	235673
8.	2003-04	246367	15226	261593
9.	2004-05	225442	9236	234678
10.	2005-06	272508	10345	282853
11.	2006-07	268743	21882	290625

Interpretation

In 1996-97 the total container handled was .210386. In ten years period its growth was steady. In 2006-07 total container handled was 2,90,625. The share of international and domestic containers in 2006-07 was 21,087 and 61507 respectively.

Table 5.2(*b*). Container Handled in Eastern Region.

Sl.No.	Year	International	Domestic	Total
1.	1996-97	8798	68298	77096
2.	1997-98	12338	50981	63319
3.	1998-99	12004	36104	48108
4.	1999-00	12930	43847	56777
5.	2000-01	14709	57055	71764
6.	2000-02	13037	59972	73009
7.	2002-03	19983	67152	87135
8.	2003-04	22005	69701	91706
9.	2004-05	31635	66491	98126
10.	2005-06	17444	63168	80612
11.	2006-07	21087	61507	82594

Interpretation

In 1996-97 the total container handled was 77096. In ten years its growth was not steady. In 2006-07 total container handled was 82,594. The share of international and domestic containers in 2006-07 were 21,087 and 61507 respectively.

Table 5.2(*c*). Container Handled in Southern Region.

Sl.No.	Year	International	Domestic	Total
1.	1996-97	106614	15177	121791
2.	1997-98	116750	18359	135109
3.	1998-99	102241	30297	132538
4.	1999-00	120734	46988	167722
5.	2000-01	130217	56162	186379
6.	2001-02	127868	64312	192180
7.	2002-03	135095	70316	205411
8.	2003-04	170941	70884	241825
9.	2004-05	184518	64025	248543
10.	2005-06	219226	69835	289061
11.	2006-07	233947	69521	303468

Interpretation

Total Container handled in 1996-07 was 1,21,791 where international and domestic containers share were 1,06,614 and 15,177. In ten years period, the total traffic increased to 303468 where share of international and domestic containers increased to 2,33,947 and 69521 respectively.

Table 5.2(*d*). Container Handled in Central Region

Sl.No.	Year	International	Domestic	Total
1.	1997-98	14552	34403	48955
2.	1998-99	14830	20344	35174
3.	1999-00	21168	5610	26778
4.	2000-01	28919	4373	33292
5.	2001-02	40418	7421	47839
6.	2002-03	47503	8304	55807
7.	2003-04	52524	11901	64425
8.	2004-05	55944	31434	87378
9.	2005-06	62196	17469	79665
10.	2006-07	77948	19203	97151

Interpretation

Total Container handled in 1997-08 was 48,955, where international and domestic containers share were 14552 and 34403. In 2006-07 it increased to 97151 where share of international and domestic container increased to 77948 and 19203 respectively.

Table 5.2(*e*) Container Handled in North Central Region

Sl.No.	Year	International	Domestic	Total
1.	2003-04	437548	117	437665
2.	2004-05	133363	17324	150687
3.	2005-06	140781	11333	152114
4.	2006-07	197821	7152	204973

Interpretation

In 2003-04 the operation began in this region. During 2003-04 total container handled were 4,37,665 where international and domestic share of containers were 4,37,548 and 117. In 2006-07 total container reduced to 2,04,973 where international container reduced to 1,97,821 and domestic container also has fluctuating rate of growth.

Table 5.2(*f*). Container Handled in Northern Region

Sl.No.	Year	International	Domestic	Total
1.	1996-96	184182	87121	271303
2.	1997-97	209158	75951	285109
3.	1998-98	248225	84719	332944
4.	1999-00	295876	92602	388478
5.	2000-01	340006	110907	450913
6.	2001-02	427572	124688	552260
7.	2002-03	505884	143607	649491
8.	2003-04	185128	144697	329825
9.	2004-05	588925	124316	713241
10.	2005-06	684343	152231	836574
11.	2006-07	732483	157132	889615

Interpretation

In 1996-97 the total container handled in this region was 2,71,303, where international and domestic containers share were 1,84,182 and 87,121 respectively. In ten years period there is growth of three and half times. In 2006-07 total container handling increased to 8,89,615 where international container increased to 7,32,483 and domestic container increased to 1,57,132.

Table 5.2(*g*). Container Handled in South Central Region

Sl.No.	Year	International	Domestic	Total
1.	1996-97	14095	8871	22966
2.	1997-98	11746	10159	21905
3.	1998-99	11452	6238	17690
4.	1999-00	14541	7597	22138
5.	2000-01	19424	17149	36573
6.	2001-02	20762	22617	43379
7.	2002-03	24290	23020	47310
8.	2003-04	32682	22776	55458
9.	2004-05	42662	25939	68601
10.	2005-06	49406	33593	82999
11.	2006-07	45594	36252	81846

Interpretation

In South Central Region the total container handled in 1996-97 was 22,966 where international container share is 14095 and domestic container no. is 8871. In ten years period the total increased to 81,846 in which share of international and domestic container handling no is 45594 and 36252 respectively.

Table 5.2(*h*). Container Handled in North-western Region

Sl.No.	Year	International	Domestic	Total
1.	2001-02	88755	30250	119005
2.	2002-03	82362	19974	102336
3.	2003-04	104423	15199	119622
4.	2004-05	114027	12695	126722
5.	2005-06	110810	15874	126684
6.	2006-07	138038	16956	154994

Interpretation

In north-western region container handling began in 2001-02. Total container handled were 1,19,005. Where international and domestic containers were 88,755 30250 respectively. In six years time container handling total figures increased to 1,54,994. International containers handled increased to 1,38,038 where domestic figures decreased to 16,956.

Table 5.3(*a*). Container Handled at ICD Tughlakabad (Delhi)/Northern Region

Sl.No.	Year	International	Domestic	Total
1.	2005-2006	405845	0	405845
2.	2006 -2007	410074	0	410074

Interpretation

The total container handled at ICD Tughlakabad (Delhi) / Northern Region ICD Tughlakabad (Delhi) Northern region in 2005-06 was 4,05,845 which increased to 4,10,074. In this container depot only international container were handled. This ICD is the best performer among all ICD and CFS of CONCOR.

Table 5.3 (*b*). Container Handled at CD DDL (Ludhiana) Northern Region

Sl.No.	Year	International	Domestic	Total
1.	2005-2006	120689	5874	126563
2.	2006-2007	127202	4144	131346

Interpretation

Container handled in this ICD during 2005-06 and 2006-07 were 1,26,563 and 1,31,346. The figures share rise in container traffic. International and domestic figures in 2005-2006 were 1,20,689 and 5,874. where in 2006-07 the international containers handled increased to 1,27,207 where domestic containers reduced to 4,144.

Table 5.3(*c*). Container Handled at DADRI / North Central Region

Sl.No.	Year	International	Domestic	Total
1.	2005-2006	96363	0	96363
2.	2006-2007	135385	0	135385

Interpretation

This ICD is at third number on the basis of total container handled. Its figures of total containers handled increased from 96,363 to 1,35,385. All figures represent international container. There is increasing trend in International container handling.

Table 5.3(*d*). Container Handled at ICD Sabarmati (Ahmedabad) / North Western Region

Sl.No.	Year	International	Domestic	Total
1.	2005-2006	96113	0	96113
2.	2006-2007	112616	0	112616

Interpretation

This ICD existing in North western region got fourth position. Total containers handled in 2005-06 were 96,113 where is 2006-07 it increased to 1,12,616. Here all containers handled were international.

Table 5.3(e). Container Handled at Container Freight Station Tondiarpet / Southern Region

Sl.No.	Year	International	Domestic	Total
1.	2005-2006	66483	44567	111050
2.	2006-2007	58369	42535	100904

Interpretation

This container Freight Station fifth on the basis of its performance in handling containers. Figures in 2005-06 were 111050 where it decreases to 100904 in 2006-07. Containers handled international and domestic in 2005-06 were 66483 and 44567. It reduced to 58369 and 42535 for international and domestic container handling during 2006-07.

Table 5.3(*f*). Container Handled at CFS Dronagiri- CONCOR-DRT (NAVI MUMBAI) / Western Region

Sl.No.	Year	International	Domestic	Total
1.	2005-2006	95133	0	95133
2.	2006-2007	106128	0	106128

Interpretation

This container Freight Station is sixth on the basis of its performance in handling containers. Figures in 2005-06 were 95133 where it increased to 106128. Containers handled international in 2005-06 were 95133. It figures increased to 106128 for international container handling during 2006-07.

Table 5.3(g). Container Handled at DCT/Okhla/ Northern Region

Sl.No.	Year	International
1.	2005-2006	0
2.	2006-2007	0

Interpretation

This ICD is seventh on the basis of its performance in handling containers. Figures in 2005-06 were 100093 where it reduced to 93650 in 2006-07.There is decrease in handling of container. Only domestic containers are handled here.

Table 5.3(h). Container Handled at Inland Container Depot Whitefield / Southern Region

Sl.No.	Year	International
1.	2005-2006	67718
2.	2006-2007	79702

Interpretation

This container Freight Station stands eighth on the basis of its performance in handling containers. Total container handled figures in 2005-06 was 87703 where it increased to 99249 in 2006-07. Containers handled international and domestic in 2005-06 were 67718 and19985. It increased to 79702 for international but reduced to 19547 in domestic container handling during 2006-07.

Table 5.3(j). Container Handled at Inland Container Depot, Nagpur / Central Region

Sl.No.	Year	International	Domestic	Total
1.	2005-2006	53284	5630	58914
2.	2006-2007	64005	11447	75452

Interpretation

This ICD is ranked ninth on the basis of its performance in handling containers. Total containers handled Figures in 2005-06 were 58914 where it increases to 75452 in 2006-07. Containers handled international and domestic in 2005-06 were 53284 and 5630 respectively. It increased to 64005 and 11447 for international and domestic container handling during 2006-07.

Table 5.3(k) Container Handled at ICD NEW Mulund (Mumbai) / Western Region

Sl.No.	Year	International	Domestic	Total
1.	2005-2006	67679	72	67751
2.	2006-2007	66524	0	66524

Interpretation

This ICD is ranked tenth on the basis of its performance in handling containers. Total containers handled figures in 2005-06 were 67751 where it reduced to 66524 in 2006-07. Containers handled international and domestic in 2005-06 were 67679 and 72 respectively. It reduced to 66524 and 0 for international and domestic container handling during 2006-07.

CONCOR Offer of Block Booking on Round Trip Basis

"Scheduled Day Service on Round Trip Basis" will be offered to shipping line / group of lines/ consolidators fro ICD Dadri from Mundra, Vizag and Pipavav. Similar Services will be considered from select CONCOR terminals to these gateway ports on request. Services to other ports like Chennai, Kolkata and Haldia ports can also be considered. The Line /Lines together will be required to pay a minimum amount for booking of a rake on round trip basis. For this, they will register with the respective terminals and open a pre-deposit account with CONCOR at the originating terminal. The necessary minimum amount may be deposited in the PDA before the start of the train.

Booking for laden and empty containers will be levied as per public tariff from the concerned shipping lines and all leviable surcharges would be added. For empty slots, CONCOR will levy the applicable empty container freight rates in the stream.

The schedule of departure and the number of services may be decided by the shipping line/ lines, which CONCOR will agree to if there are no serious operational constraints. Occasional request for rescheduling of a particular service may be accommodated, provided such request is received at least one day prior to the scheduled departure of the train from ICD. The train will be run with onhand containers following FIFO.

The same rake as would carry export volumes to port will bring back import boxes for the same line/ consolidator. The necessary loading at port end has to be tied up with the port terminal operator by the consolidator/ Shipping line.

Since the shipping line may also act as a consolidator by accepting volumes offered by other lines to top up their own volumes in order to fill up all the slots in a particular train, the forwarding note must have the endorsement of the consolidating line indicating that booking is against the block train scheme. However, IW Bills for loaded and empty containers will be raised as per normal procedure by debiting the concerned shipping line's PDA.

CONCOR will have the right to fill up empty slots if wagons are running empty from ICD/ port. However, in such cases CONCOR will not charge for the empty slots, utilised by CONCOR provided at least 45 laden TEUs have been booked by line / consolidator. At the pot end, the train will not be detained on account of non-availability of containers.

Discount admissible will be paid after monthly reconciliation of the figures, on the round trips completed. Discount will be payable on total amount realised against laden booking, provided at least 90 loaded TEUs have been booked on round trip basis. The discount may be paid in the form of a refund, through PDA.

Non-dedicated 'common services' to Mundra, Pipava and Vizag ports will continue to run regularly, the frequency of which will be intimated from time to time.

LCL Consolidation

The process of LCL consolidation involves the movement of less than container load cargo from an Inland Container Deport to a nominated 'hub' terminal under customs seal, usually in a domestic container of some sort. At the nominated hub terminal, the sealed containers are opened and the cargo re-worked on a destination wise basis without having to be subjected to re-examination by customs. Indian Customs permitted the reworking of LCL boxes in certain nominated 'hub terminals' mostly located at port cities in the year 2000.

This has already led to a tremendous increase in the business of LCL consolidation in the country. Export LCL consolidation of different ICDs' custom cleared cargo, often along with locally cleared LCL cargo makes for must faster clearance of cargo, and reduces the end to end transit times between the originating points and destinations of the cargo being moved.

Reduced transit times of LCL hub movements have provided opportunity to shippers to move their LCL consignments faster, at extremely cost effective LCL sea tariffs. Due to the reworking of such cargo at nominated hub points within India, direct destination sailings to USA, Europe, Africa, Gulf etc., become available via the Mumbai/ Chennai transshipment HUBs. This also reduces the sea transits for LCL movements, which otherwise have to face a more expensive transshipment at locations like Singapore or Colombo.

CONCOR currently provides LCL consolidation services from various locations such as Agra, Moradabad, Kanpur, Dhandari Kalan (Ludhiana), Whitefield (Bangalore), Tondiarpet (Chennai), Sanathnagar (Secundrabad), Sabarmati (Ahmedabad), Nagpur, Aurangabad, Mulund (Mumbai) and Pithampur (Indore).

CONCOR's ICDs at Tondiarpet (Chennai) and Mulund-East (Mumbai) have been nominated as 'Hub' points for transshipment. In addition, a substantial amount of traffic is also moved between hinterland terminals and the hub points at the Maersk's CWC's CFSs at Dronagiri Node in Mumbai. While most of the movements of LCL consolidation cargo are road based, in the case of very long lead, CONCOR has even made the arrangement of moving the containers by rail up to Mumbai, and re-positioning them locally by road to Dronagiri for reconsolidation.

Some of the Special Features of this Service from different Locations Are:

Most of the services move on fixed road schedules, to ensure connectivity with ship sailing from the gateway ports after reconsolidation at CFSs/terminals at Gateway Ports. The cargo is moved either in close body trucks or domestic containers. Some forwarders are also moving the cargo in their own containers. CONCOR has earmarked separate space for consolidation and de-consolidation activities in its existing warehouses, and plans to continue doing so in the new warehouses being developed. CONCOR acts as Custodian of cargo up to the HUBs (Re-working Places) in India *i.e.,* CFS, Mulund/ CFS, Dronagiri, CFS/Tondiarpet. At the HUBs, the LCL consolidator presents both the copies of Shipping Bill to the proper officer of Customs who verifies the genuineness of documents and checks the marks and numbers of the seal on the trucks/containers as recorded on the documents. CONCOR has already executed bonds for the transport of goods from various ICDs to "HUBs" and vice versa.[6]

For exports, all customs formalities relating to cargo examination etc. are completed prior to the movement of cargo. Shippers have to give a copy of the invoice and packing list of each shipping bill, to be checked at the consolidation terminal, and subsequently forwarded to the hub centre. CONCOR issues a delivery order to each of the parties to enable them to collect the cargo from hub centre.

For import cargo, consolidators are required to hand over LCL consignments for a particular destination to CONCOR at the hub terminal after completing customs formalities relating to transhipment at the hub point. Thereafter, CONCOR carries the cargo to destination and arranges delivery of cargo after its customs examination etc. at the nominated ICD. Bills of entry are required to be filed only at the destination ICDs. Each party *i.e.* CHAs, consolidators, shipping lines has to issue a separate delivery order to their customers at the ICDs, which is required to be surrendered at the time of delivery of cargo.

CONCOR accepts LCL cargoes from CHAs, consolidators, shipping lines irrespective of the volume of the cargo available with each of them.

Air Cargo Division

In pursuance of its objective to provide improved Intermodal logistics solutions to India's trade, CONCOR entered the field of air cargo in 1999. The Air Cargo business was formalised as a division at the Corporate Office in 2003 to provide a focussed attention.

CONCOR undertakes various Air Cargo activities as follows:

1. Road feeder services
   (*a*) Airports to airports
   (*b*) Airports to Inland Container Depots/Container Freight Station
2. Air Freight Station in ICD/CFS.
3. Centres for Perishable Cargo.
4. Bonded warehousing for imports at its ICDs/CFSs.
5. Air Cargo Complex at Ozhar Airport, Nasik and old Airport, Banglore.

Road Feeder Services

CONCOR has obtained requisite permission from customs at major international airports as well as at 49 other ICDs spread across the country for movement of export/import cargo under bond. CONCOR currently provides road feeder services from Delhi, Mumbai, Agra, Kanpur, Ludhiana, Moradabad, Jaipur, Whitefield (Bangalore), Chennai, Sanathnagar (Secundrabad), Kolkata, Sabarmati (Ahmedabad), Nagpur, Aurangabad, Pithampur (Indore) etc. This service is proposed to be expanded to other places as well.

Air Cargo Complexes and Centres for Perishable Cargo

CONCOR has opened a greenfield Cargo Complex at Ozhar Airport, Nasik, jointly with Hindustan Aeronautics Limited

(HAL). The complex has an air cargo facility, sea cargo facility and a Centre for Perishable Cargo (CPC) for direct international airlifting from/to Nasik Airport. CONCOR is also constructing a 'Packhouse'—centre for sorting, grading, packing and precooling of vegetables and fruits prior to export, at Nasik.

CONCOR has constructed a another CPC at Goa Airport to promote the perishable cargo trade.

Bonded and Other Warehousing

Air imports desiring deferred payment of duty are offered customs-bonded warehousing facility at our ICDs. This is a thriving business at ICD/Whitefield at Bangalore. Bonded warehousing is available at other ICDs as well. (a list of CONCOR's ICDs can be seen elsewhere for information). Warehouses can also be offered on leave and licence basis, wherever available. Air cargo is growing the world over. CONCOR plans to move hand in hand with this growth by steadily increasing its facilitation to the air cargo trade by participating in other activities as well.

Reefer Services

Reefers, or Refrigerated containers facilitate the movement of cargo that requires a strict temperature controlled environment. Running of Reefer services requires a certain degree of Infrastructure development at the handling terminals, and CONCOR has made such facilities available at its terminals, *i.e.* ICD Dadri and ICD Kanpur.

The Reefer containers are moved from the terminal to the factories for stuffing on special trailers, on which a 'clip on' generator can be attached to supply power to the Reefer units. On return to the ICD, they are stacked at a nominated location with special facilities for plugging in the containers to uninterrupted power sources, and regular temperature monitoring.

The reefer containers are moved on High Speed 'BLCA' wagons between ICD Dadri and JNPT/NSICT/GTIL ports in Mumbai. The power to the units while on run is provided from specially designed power packs which are fitted in modified 40 ft containers, and loaded on the trains. Each power pack serves upto 22 FEUs, and CONCOR is currently operating full rakes wih reefer containers.

CONCOR is also moving domestic reefer containers from ICD Dadri and Kanpur to domestic terminal at Turbhe. CONCOR has plans to offer these services from other terminals as well subject to materialisation of adequate traffic levels.

Factory Stuffing/Destuffing

Keeping in time with the international trend, containers are now going to shipper's units more and more for cargo stuffing/ destuffing, as against the general trend a decade earlier, when most of the cargo was getting stuffed/destuffed at the ports/ ICDs. CONCOR's ICDs are now fully geared to provide the requisite "on-carriage" and "pre-carriage" facilities to shippers, hence fully eliminating any cargo handling en route. While such facilities are often available through private channels, CONCOR also has arrangements for providing such services on-demand at competitive rates as part of its efforts to provide single-window services. Details regarding these services as well as rates etc. can be ascertained directly from the personnel at various ICDs.

Discount Schemes

CONCOR has special incentive schemes operating at some of its terminals keeping in tune with the existing business trends. Special volume linked incentives are also on offer to shipping lines and exporters. Some of the schemes in vogue are as under:

1. Volume Discount Scheme in Imports to Shipping Lines based on the import containers booked by them from the gateway ports to CONCOR ICDs on CONCOR trains.

2. Volume Discount scheme for rice exporters booking containers from CONCOR's terminals at ICD Tughlakabad, Dadri, Rewari, Sonepat and Ludhiana.

Terminal-Specific schemes are also on offer at various terminals like Jaipur, Jodhpur, Moradabad, Tondiarpet, Whitefield, Dronagiri Node, Pithampur etc.

Cabotage of ISO Containers

Extensive movement of shipping-line empty containers is undertaken by CONCOR to balance the differential levels of exports and imports in the country today. This movement of empty containers represents a wasted capacity, especially on routes where substantial domestic traffic is available for parallel movement by road or even on rail. In order to optimise the use of its resources, CONCOR offers the facility of 'cabotage' to shipping lines who wish to move empty containers as balancing movements. A 'cabotaged' container is effectively loaned by the shipping company to the carrier (in this case CONCOR) for a very short period (usually a single one way trip). During this trip, the carrier is permitted to use the container for movement of domestic cargo. By 'cabotaging' these containers, CONCOR can therefore offer a substantial discount to both shipping lines and the potential domestic client. This is seen as an area of focus and strategy to boost volumes and profitability.

CONCOR regularly offers Cabotage services on it's core exim route between Mumbai and Delhi. In addition, such services are also available on demand for other movements, subject to the availability of adequate domestic traffic volumes. Since CONCOR does not possess any 40 ft. containers in its domestic fleet, all domestic movements in 40 ft. containers is done by cabotaging international 40 ft. containers.

Door Delivery and Pick-ups

One of the prime objectives of the domestic division is to bring back to rail, goods which are now being transported by road.

A key business thrust that has been made by the company in the area of domestic business has been in seeking to pick up such traffic that is moving by road by offering door-to-door pick-up and delivery services

The concept of door pick-ups and delivery takes us one step closer to achieving the primary objective of becoming a truly multi-modal logistics service provider. We are also seeking to make the process of delivery and pick-up as simple as possible so that all the necessary paper work can be completed at the customer's door, and the customer need not visit the terminal at all.

In certain cases, we have even made arrangements for the unloading of cargo from containers, and the delivery of loose cargo if this the customer's requirements. We are also in close touch with our customers to ensure that deliveries are made as far as possible according to their convenience and requirements.

Rating of door delivery and pick-ups is normally done on the basis of slab rates. The following table is indicative of the additional costs over and above the rail transport and handling costs that have to be incurred for availing of this service. Rating of door delivery and pick-ups is normally done on the basis of slab rates. The following table is indicative of the additional costs over and above the rail transport and handling costs that have to be incurred for availing of this service.

Table 5.4 (*a*) Door Delivery and Pick-up Rates (For Local Transportation)

TNPM

Distance		Weight		Rate
From	**To**	**From**	**To**	**2450**
1	10	0	20.7	2850
11	20	0	20.7	3300
21	30	0	20.7	55
For Every KM above 30 KM				2450

Table 5.4 (*b*). DCT Okhla Tuglakabad (TKD)

Distance		Rate/For Weight Up to 20.7 MT		Rate/For Weight > 20.7 to 25.7 MT	Rate/For Weight >25.7 to 27.5 MT
From	To	Stuffing	Destuffing	Stuffing/ Destuffing	Stuffing/ Destuffing
0	20	3200	3300	3450	3850
21	30	3500	3500	3750	4250
31	40	3750	3650	4100	4650
41	50	4050	3950	4450	5050
51	60	4400	4350	4800	5450
61	70	4700	4650	5150	5850
71	80	5050	4950	5550	6650
81	90	5350	5250	5900	6650
91	100	5700	5550	6250	7100
101	110	6050	6050	6600	7500
111	120	6400	6400	7000	7900
121	130	6700	6700	7300	8300
131	140	7050	7050	7650	8700
141	150	7400	7400	8000	9100
151	175	8150	8150	8950	10150
176	200	9000	9000	9900	11250
201	225	9900	9900	10850	12300
226	250	10750	10750	11800	13400
251	275	11600	11600	12750	14500
276	300	12450	12450	13700	15500
301	325	13350	13350	14650	16650
326	350	14200	14200	15600	17700
351	375	15050	15050	16550	18800
376	400	15900	15900	17500	19850

For movement to Uttaranchal and Himanchal : above 150 kms an additional add on charges od Rs. 300/- 25 kms per 20'/22/ container, will be collected.

Table 5.4 (*c*) Nagpur Tariff (NGP)

Distance		Weight		Rate	
From	To	From	To	Stuffing	Destuffing
0	20	0	21.7	3700	3800
0	20	21.8	25.7	4000	4200
0	20	25.8	27.5	4500	4600
For Every 10 KM above 20 KM				800	800

Table 5.4 (*d*). Concor Tariff CNTR Fright STTN Vishakhapatnam (CFCV)

Distance		Stuffing/De-stuffing	Size/ Rate in Rs.	
From	To		20' Cntr	40' Cntr
Upto	15 Kms	Upto 20.7 in 20′ & 19.3 Mt in 40′	1735	2205
		Rate per tonne beyond above specified weight catageory	190	245
16	30 Kms	Upto 20.7 in 20′ & 19.3 Mt in 40′	2785	3320
		Rate per tonne beyond above specified weight catageory	225	255
31	45 Kms	Upto 20.7 in 20′ & 19.3 Mt in 40′	3540	4675
		Rate per tonne beyond above specified weight catageory	240	375
Add on charges for every 10 Kms beyond 45 Km		Upto 20.7 in 20′ & 19.3 Mt in 40′	770	875
		Rate per tonne beyond above specified weight catageory	275	390

Table 5.4 (*e*) Concor Tariff Terminal Coal Dock Rd (Kolkata) (CTKR)

Distance		Weight/ Cntr 20		Weight/ Cntr40
From	To	1-20.07	20.7-27.5	27 MT
1	10	2500	3000	4800
For each block of 5 km beyond up to 85 kms		500	600	600

Table 5.4 (f). Ankleshwar (AKV)

Distance		Cntr 20′ Up to 21.7 MT	Cntr 20′ Cntr 40′ Upto 19.3 MT
From	To	Stuffing/De-stuffing	
>20	30 kms	2000	3500
>30	40 kms	4000	4600
>40	50 kms	4900	5600
> 50 Kms on Per km Basis (Upto 150 kms		60	65

Table 5.4 (g). Kanakpura, Jaipur (KKU)

Distance		Stuffing/ De-stuffing		Stuffing/ De-stuffing		Stuffing/ De-stuffing	
From	To	20′ Upto 20.7 T	40′ Upto 19.3 T	20′ >20.7 <=25.7 T	40′ >19.3 <=24.3 T	20′ >25.7 <=27.5 T	40′ >24.3 <=27 T
Upto	20 Kms	1540	2080	1694	2288	1925	2600
21	30	1930	2470	2123	2717	2413	3088
31	40	2320	2860	2552	3146	2900	3575
41	50	2710	3250	2981	3575	3388	4063
51	60	3100	3640	3410	4004	3875	4550
61	70	3490	4030	3839	4433	4363	5038
71	80	3880	4420	4268	4862	4850	5525
81	90	4270	4810	4697	5291	5338	6013
91	100	4660	5200	5126	5720	5825	6500
101	125	5510	6050	6061	6655	6888	7563
126	150	6360	6900	6996	7590	7950	8625
151	175	7210	7750	7931	8525	9013	9688
176	200	8060	8600	8866	9460	10075	10750
201	225	8910	9450	9801	10395	11138	11813
226	250	9760	10300	10736	11330	12200	12875
251	275	10610	11150	11671	12265	13263	13938
276	300	11460	12000	12606	13200	14325	15000

FS=Factory Stuffing
FDS=Factory De-stuffing
Weight=Cargo Weight Only[8]

Cabotage of ISO Container

Extensive movement of shipping-line empty containers is undertaken by CONCOR to balance the differential levels of exports and imports in the country today. This movement of empty containers represents a wasted capacity, especially on routes where substantial domestic traffic is available for parallel movement by road or even on rail. In order to optimise the use of its resources, CONCOR offers the facility of 'cabotage' to shipping lines who wish to move empty containers as balancing movements. A 'cabotaged' container is effectively loaned by the shipping company to the carrier (in this case CONCOR) for a very short period (usually a single one way trip). During this trip, the carrier is permitted to use the container for movement of domestic cargo. By 'cabotaging' these containers, CONCOR can therefore offer a substantial discount to both shipping lines and the potential domestic client. This is seen as an area of focus and strategy to boost volumes and profitability.

CONCOR regularly offers Cabotage services on it's core exim route between Mumbai and Delhi. In addition, such services are also available on demand for other movements, subject to the availability of adequate domestic traffic volumes. Since CONCOR does not possess any 40 ft. Containers in its domestic fleet, all domestic movements in 40 ft. containers is done by cabotaging international 40 ft. containers.

Volume Discount Schemes

In order to encourage domestic traffic on certain streams, CONCOR follows a policy of announcing a series of volume based discount schemes. These schemes are basically aimed at sharing some of the benefits of lower costs achieved by the company due to higher volumes offered by the customers. These schemes are usually announced for fixed streams up to a definite validity period, with a telescopic effect in terms of the benefits offered. The discount per TEU will normally increase as the overall voulme increases. The discounts are usually offered in the form of a rebate that is given after a customer has successfully completed the specified volumes.

Volume Discount for very high slabs (usually more than 300 TEUs) are sometimes made available to customers who enter into an agreement with CONCOR committing the volume. Customers who commit volumes can be given the discounted rate at the time of booking, but in case the customer falls short of the committed volume, dead freight is levied on the shortfall. These schemes are basically aimed at sharing some of the benefits of lower costs achieved by the company due to higher volumes offered by the customers.

These schemes are usually announced for fixed streams up to a definite validity period, with a telescopic effect in terms of the benefits offered. The discount per TEU will normally increase as the overall voulme increases. The discounts are usually offered in the form of a rebate that is given after a customer has successfully completed the specified volumes.

Volume Discount for very high slabs (usually more than 300 TEUs) are sometimes made available to customers who enter into an agreement with CONCOR committing the volume. Customers who commit volumes can be given the discounted rate at the time of booking, but in case the customer falls short of the committed volume, dead freight is levied on the shortfall.

Terminal Network of CONCOR

CONCOR operates through its terminal, the region in which it is located are given below:[8]

Northern Region

Tughlakabad(Delhi), Panipat, Moradabad, ICD DDL (Ludhiana), Ballabgarh, Jaipur, Jodhpur, Rewari, DCT/TKD, Kharia Khangar, Gotan, DCT Phillaur, Moga, Gurgaon (Planned), Sonepat, Dhappar, Surnasi (Under Construction), Khemli (Planned)

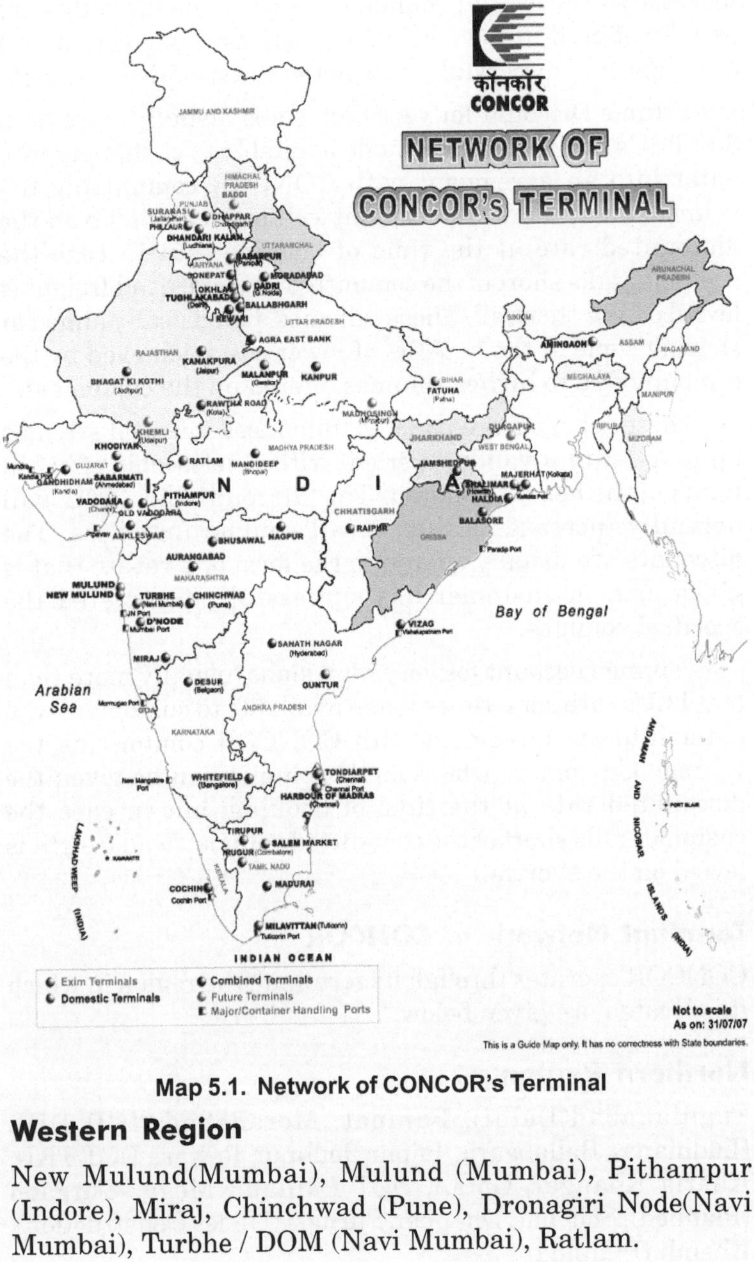

Map 5.1. Network of CONCOR's Terminal

Western Region

New Mulund(Mumbai), Mulund (Mumbai), Pithampur (Indore), Miraj, Chinchwad (Pune), Dronagiri Node(Navi Mumbai), Turbhe / DOM (Navi Mumbai), Ratlam.

Eastern Region

Amingaon (Guwahati), Shalimar (Kolkata), Majerhat (CTKR), Kolkata Port (Kolkata), Jamshedpur, Haldia, Fatuha (Patna), Balasore.

Southern Region

Whitefield (Bangalore), Irugur, Tondiarpet(Chennai), Madurai, Harbour of Chennai (HOM), Cochin (CHTS), Milavittan(Tuticorin), Salem Market/DOM, Tiruppur.

Central Region

Nagpur / Daulatabad (Aurangabad) / Bhusawal/ Raipur / Mandideep.

South Central Regions

Sanatnagar(Hyderabad), Guntur, Visakhapatnam, Desur.

REFERENCES

1. *Containerisation, Multi-modal Transport and Infrastructure Development in India* by Dr KV Hariharan, Shroff Publication, New Delhi 2005.
2. *Annual Reports of CONCOR,* Published Annually by CONCOR, New Delhi, 2007.
3. Hand book on Multi modal Transport (Containerisation) and Logistics Management, Institute of Rail Transport, New Delhi, 2004.
4. *Annual Reports of CONCOR, Published Annually by CONCOR,* New Delhi, 2007.
5. *Annual Reports of CONCOR, Published Annually by CONCOR,* New Delhi, 2007.
6. *Hand Book on Multi-modal Transport (Containerisation) and Logistics Management,* Institute of Rail Transport, New Delhi, 2004.
7. www.concorindia.com.
8. www.concorindia.com.

Marketing Practices in CONCOR

Chapter 6

INTRODUCTION

Marketing is as old as civilisation. Though marketing is talked and discussed in business terms today, its origin goes back to the ancient civilisation when man used symbols, signs and material artifacts to transact and communicate the others. Modern marketing revolves around the concepts, which are age old. The first signs that man made to communicate with others gave birth to the idea of marketing.

On popular note, marketing happened from the first time when Adam was able to communicate with Eve and there was an exchange of emotion, love, care and passion. Though there was no profit motive there was a substantial exchange for initial benefit between both the parties. Ever since then whenever there was surplus of possessions or outputs, people started exchanging them for the products of their choice.

It was only after 1945 that advertising agencies began to define the discipline in a way which came close to the modern marketing concept. Discipline matured in the 1970s, led by Phillip Kotler's seminal text. Marketing Management, first published in 1967 in which the idea of marketing evolved from practice to a discipline of learning. Marketing became re-utilised as a key management.[1]

In the 1980s, marketing moved on to the service industries, particularly retailing and financial services industries, which were experiencing massive changes.

There was a bigger revolution in the offing in the form of Internet. Due to the advent of Internet, distance between the buyer and seller became negligible and technology aided in facilitating transactions more accurately. Company started building up marketing decision support systems, in which a part of the system managed delivery (service delivery system) and another part (analytical system) helped in analysing e-commerce and m-commerce platforms to reach and serve customer better.

Today, marketing is a key function of management. It brings success to business organisation. A business organisation performs two key functions *i.e.* producing goods and services and making them available to the potential customers for use. An organisation's business success largely depends on how efficiently the products and services are delivered to the customers and how differently the customers perceive the difference in delivery in comparison to the competitors. This is true of all firms from large business enterprises to small firms, from multinational operating in different countries to small firms operating in a small market.

Marketing brings liquidity and measurable business success to the organisation. Marketing is the fundamental pillar for achieving business goals.

DEVELOPING MARKETING ORIENTATION

It is understood that one needs to have marketing orientation in the organisation, failing which it will be difficult to satisfy customers over a longer period of time. But managers are not aware of methods and techniques by which they can reorient their organisations into marketing-oriented organisations. Successful development of a marketing orientation requires a thorough understanding of the organisation's existing culture and a carefully constructed programme of management development, support activates and follow-up to overcome the organisational inertia that can impede the transition to marketing effectiveness.

A programme to increase market orientation can be developed by understanding the mix of potentially conflicting orientations in the organisations, identifying the present levels of marketing effectiveness and implementing a plan to improve the marketing orientation. When need to understands the range of conflicting orientations that run in different organisations. Product oriented companies feel that their product sells in the market because the quality of the product will pull customers. Cost-oriented managers believe that the only way to improve profits is to reduce marketing and production costs. Capacity oriented companies believe that the more they make, the more profitable they are and if they go into the market with more variants, customers will buy them. Erratic oriented firms believe that no planning is possible for future because nobody knows what is going to happen in the future. A marketing oriented company makes profit by creating opportunities to satisfy more effectively the customer needs witching the constraints of its resources and skill limitations. Conducting workshops, and indepth interviews of senior management, can identify these orientations.

Phillip Kotler has identified five attributes that combine to form the marketing effectiveness of a company. They are customer philosophy, integrated marketing organisation, adequate marketing information, strategic orientation and operational efficiency.

Customer philosophy, identifies the extent to which the management acknowledges the importance of the market and customer needs in shaping the plans and operations of the company, Integrated marketing. Organisation analysis should find out to what extent the organisation is staffed for marketing analysis, planning, implementation and control. The marketing manager can identify to what extent the management receive quality market information necessary to conduct an effective marketing programme.

LOGISTICS MARKETING—THE CONCEPT

The term Logistics marketing is identification of the most profitable markets now and in future, assessing the present and future needs of the users, setting business development goals and making plans to meet them and further managing the services and promoting them to achieve the plans all in the context of the changing business environmental conditions to cater to the changing socio-economic needs. It is a managerial device to formulate marketing mix which makes possible an optimal utilisation of the marketing resources to fulfill the changing needs and requirements of general as well as the industrial users. It consider's marketing customer satisfaction engineering and therefore the professionals bear the responsibility of making marketing decisions with the prime motto of satisfying the users. In addition, the marketing decisions make ways for the designing of a rational fare and freight structure that helps the transport organisations in maintaining the commercial viability. Besides, it is a managerial process to bridge over the gap between the services-promised and services-offered.

The aforesaid facts make it clear that the term Logistics marketing is application of marketing principles by the transport organisations in which the marketing professionals make sincere efforts to market the services in such a way that generation of profit, satisfaction to users and protection of social interests are made easier. Since we find the business environment more competitive, the marketing decisions help in excelling competition by making the services internationally completive. It is a device that makes the ways for development and expansion. Since we find all decisions clustering around customers/users, the transport marketing proves to be a device to study the changing behavioural profile of both the categories as users. At the same time, we find transport marketing helping an organisation in making profits but in no case, we find a place for profiteering. We use profit as a tantamount of profiteering but both the terms have a diriment meaning and implications. The Logistics generating organisations have a legitimate right of making profits since this simplifies the task of improving the quality of services and fulfilling the needs and requirements. A caged bird can't lay eggs of normal size. In the transport marketing or generally in the service generating organisations when we talk about making of profits, it focus on profit making by promoting fair, ethical and legitimate practices. Profit that engineers a sound foundation of development and expansions helps in satisfying the users.

The marketing concept in CONCOR focuses on some of the important problems as mentioned below:[3]

- It is managerial device to promote the *Logistics* business.
- It helps the *Logistics* generating organisations in making profits
- It is a device to shape the perception of customer satisfaction.
- It is an effort to excel competition.
- It is a social process that makes a strong advocacy in favour of sub serving the social interests.
- It is an attempt to make available world class *Logistics* services to the end users.
- It is an organised effort to promote business.

USERS OF LOGISTICS SERVICE

In the Logistics generating organisations or even in other service generating organisations, it is pertinent that the users are given due weightage. The different categories of users use the services with different motives. The industrial users like safe, time-honoured and economic services and like this, the industrial or organisational users also prefer quality and fast services even if they are asked to pay more. We are well aware of the fact in the Indian perspective both the public and private sectors have been found offering *Logistics* services to the general and industrial users. In Figure 6.1, the different categories of users make it clear that in the service generating organisations like the sate Road transport Corporations, Indian Railways, Indian Airlines and Air India we find individual and general customers using the service.[2]

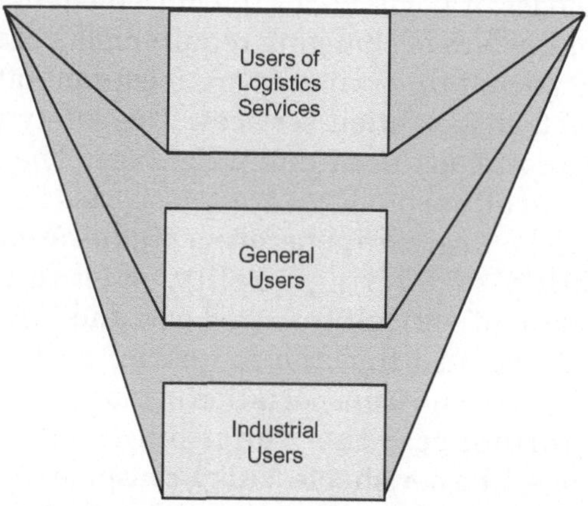

Fig. 6.1 Diagram on Logistics Services Users

General Users

In this group, we include all users rural actions availing the services of *Logistics* organisations for travelling or other purposes. Here, the potential users of the services like time-honoured and cost-effective services. The masses use different modes of transport and for the same, they are to be charged. An individual prefers to have fast, safe and economic services. The rural users/prospects avail the services with the prime motto of getting the services linked to the urban markets so that they succeed in getting a profitable return for their goods and services. In addition, they also use the passenger services. Sophistication is not an essential consideration for the rural users. On the other hand, the urban users/prefer to avail quality services containing sophistication and offering to them more comforts and conveniences.

Industrial Users

The industrial users avail the service of transport organisations with the motives of safe, economic and time honoured transportation of their goods to the destination. With the development of primary, secondary and tertiary sector, we find a significant increase in the requirements of industrial users. The agricultural sector uses the services of different modes of *Logistics* for the movement of inputs and outputs. In the face of changing requirements of this sector, it is pertinent that the transport organisations offer to them world class transportation services. The safety provisions, insurance provisions need due weightage. The perishable and other agriculture produces are transported from one place to another. The *Logistics* generating organisations bear the responsibility of offering quality, safe and economic transportation of agricultural produces and inputs. On the other hand, we also find the industrial sector using the *Logistics* service. The transportation of industrial inputs and outputs influences the functioning of industrial organisations. The perishable, bulky, consumer durables and non-durables, plants and equipments needs care of the transport organisations. Since we find different categories of industrial users availing the *Logistics* services, it is pertinent that the transport organisations assign due weightage to the interests of cottage and small industries. The subsidised and cost-based services need due attention of transport organisations. The trade and commerce sector can't work smoothly if we find *Logistics* organisations not working satisfactorily. The development of market, arrival and departure ratio of inputs and outputs, the demand and supply position would adversely be affected if the transport organisations fail in making available the quality, time-honoured, safe and economic services to the trade and commerce sector of the economy.

Behavioural Profile of Users

We are well aware of the fact that the transport organisation also need to intensify an indepth study of the behavioural profile of different categories of users so that they succeed in satisfying them. Business goes where it is invited but stays where it is well treated. For the development of an organisation or for expanding the transportation network both in the backward and developed areas, it is essential that the transport professional study the changing behavioural profile.

There is no doubt in it that the Indian Railways are the main artery of the nation's inland transport and Asia's largest and world' number one railway system under a single management. However we find enough scope of initiating qualitative-cum-quantitative transformation to cater to the changing requirements of the users.

This draws our attention on the following :

- Formulation of a sound service mix for the Indian Railways which make available to the users' world class passenger and goods traffic services.
- Promoting the services with the help of innovative measures to inform sense and persuade the users that they are offering the world calls services at a reasonable fare and freight structure.
- Offering promised services to the end users and bridging over the gap between the services-promised and services-offered.
- Rationalising the fair and freight structures so that the commercial viability is maintained.
- Developing quality personnel for the Indian Railways who are supposed to be personally committed and value-based.
- Adding additional attractions to the services so that the Indian Railways prove and continue to be number one.

THE INDIAN RAILWAYS PRODUCT

Product is anything that can be offered to market for attention, acquisition, use or consumption which includes physical objects, services, personalities, places and ideas or anything else that has the capacity to provide the satisfaction, use of perhaps the profit desired by the customers/users. The main products of Indian Railways are services which have been defined as any activity or benefit that one party can offer to another that is essentially intangible and does not result in the ownership of anything. Although some of the products are also tangible like coaches, wagons, locomotive and tracks, the emphasis here is one the marketing of services since all the tangible products are used as inputs and the ultimate outputs are the passenger and freight traffic operation made available to the end users.

In the case of freight traffic, it is between the rate of growth in Gross Domestic Product and the rate of increases in Net Tonne kms. To meet the colossal task of moving substantially higher volume of freight traffic by the year 2010 AD, the Indian Railways have to make considerable efforts to make possible an increase in the capacity.

Planning of Freight Traffic

With the pace of economic growth picking up, the Indian Railways were called upon to prove a much higher and stronger infrastructural support to the national economy. The mounting contributions of Indian Railways to the emancipation of national economy has made it significant that the tempo is maintained. Of course, the growth is unparalleled, however the increasing developmental activities make a strong advocacy in favour of enriching the potentials. Always to touch the new heights should be our slogan. While one side of the coin narrates its positive contributions, another side confirms shortages of wagons, increased cases of theft and pilferages and unfair practices influencing the financial health of Indian Railways adversely.

The agricultural and industrial development activates are inextricably interwoven with the development and fortunes of Indian Railways. In this context, the availability of wagon occupies a place of significance. To be able to cope with the pattern of traffic offering.

It is right to mention that the Indian Railways have taken certain measures to arrest diversification of traffic to road to some extents by introducing various users-friendly services, such as Domestic Container Services, Freight Forwarder Scheme, Quick Transit Scheme, Speed link Express Trains, Street Collection of so. While planning for the freight traffic, it is essential that the wagon producing units promote research to improve the quality of wagons.

What Product of Offer

Railways main products are fare and fright traffic services. Of course some of the products of the Indian Railways are tangible but we find them inputs not the outputs for the Indian Railways. A few of the public sector undertakings under the Ministry of Railways are engaged in manufacturing locomotives, coaches and wagons. What product to offer is of course a dynamic concept that changes its shape in the face of multi-dimensional development? Yesterday, the users were found satisfied with the ordinary wooden seats, today they expect cushioned seats. Yesterday, they were satisfied with the drinking water facilities to day they expect water refrigeration facilities. Yesterday, they did not make a demand for container services, today they expect.

Price Mix

Pricing decisions occupy a place of outstanding significance, especially in a utility undertaking. To be more specific in countries like ours, we find this component of the marketing complicating the tasks of professionals. Making available the rail transportation facilities to the masses and strengthening the infrastructural base for an all round development of the country can't be possible unless railways contribute substantially to the development process.

LOGISTICS MARKETING IN THE INDIAN PERSPECTIVE

Marketing Rail Transportation Services

In the modern age, we can't think about a self-sufficient society. We depend on one another and the process of dependence is likely to continue since we find a frequent change in our needs and requirements, preference, likes and dislikes attitudes, lifestyles and expectations. Transportation has proved to be an indispensable part of culture and hallmark of civilisation. Manufacturing, merchandising, banking, extracting and the like businesses substantially depend on the quality of transport services made available to the process of development. It is against this background that we need a well managed transport system which proves to be a catalyst of socio-economic transformation. Of late, we consider transport as a d facto barometer of social, economic, commercial and cultural advances. In the developing countries like ours, it is pertinent that the transportation system is created by means of a suitable network of backward and forward linkages.

DIMENSIONS OF CONCOR MARKETING PRACTICES

The business transaction is mainly between various types of industries and business houses and service organisations. Hence, it is invariably formal arrangement with detailed terms and conditions by way of contract or purchase order. In large number of case the purchase order will be of one of two pages. In case of project work, heavy machinery and high value and high volume sales the purchase documentation with detailed terms and conditions and may run to be in hundreds of pages. This is essential to bind both the parties at every stage of the project for flow of money on one side and work progress on the other side.

Marketing at CONCOR deals with technology, quality evaluation, differed payments and after sales services. Domestic and global competition is part of the business and ups and downs for' capital goods' is common.

Fewer buyers : CONCOR normally deals with far fewer buyers than any consumer marketer do.

Large value buyer : CONCOR markets are characterised by a high buyer's concentration ratio. A few large buyers do most of the purchasing.

Close supplier-customer relationship : Because of the smaller customer share and the importance and power of the larger customers there is a close relationship between customer and CONCOR. CONCOR is frequently expected to customise its offerings to individual business customer needs.

Geographically concentrated buyers : CONCOR markets are concentrated in certain Industrial belts for example Western India. Most agriculture output comes from few states of India.

Price mix : Pricing decisions occupy a place of outstanding significance in CONCOR's overall marketing domain. To be more specific in countries like ours, we find this component of the marketing complicating the tasks of professionals.

Channel Characteristics

Industrial buyers often buy directly from manufacturers rather than through intermediaries, equally those items that are technically complex and/or expensive. Consumer markets are characterised by multiple layers of intermediaries.

Promotional Characteristics

In Industrial marketing more emphasis is given to direct selling or personal selling as a relationship needs to be forged between the buyer and seller and also since there might exist technical details to be elaborated.

Unlike Industrial marketing, consumer promotions are mainly through advertising price cuts, discounts, coupons, games, etc. Advertising also helps in Industrial marketing and its through trade journal or business magazines like Business India, Business World, etc.

Pricing

In logistics marketing, price is one of the critical factors in purchase decisions. Competitive bidding and price negotiations are, very common in Industrial marketing. The payment and other commercial terms are also negotiated at the time of price negotiations. In consumer marketing the products are sold through the retailers to the consumers based on the price list of the manufacturers or the maximum retail price (MRP) for the packaged products. Sometimes, depending on the intensity of the competition the retailer reduces the price by passing on to the consumer a part of his profit.

THE INDUSTRIAL MARKETING CONCEPT

The industrial products market consist of all the organization that acquire goods and service used in production of others products or services that are sold or supplied to others. Not only are the products more technically inclined there exists a closer relationship between the customer-supplier. Hence, marketing plays a key role in the success of an Industrial products.

They must be aware of the market segmentation concepts pertaining to industrial products, the buying process as well as the decision-making process of the buying organisation. They must keep track of client objectives, competitive development, social responsibilities and regulatory development. A product centered person who is technically centered only cannot be successful. Many organisations today tend to be technically inclined or worse still financially inclined (interested greatly in cost cutting). Which leads to an organisation having excellent products but no market.

The marketing department of the organisation ensures customer satisfaction and portrays the organisation and its products to the world. Customer educations alone cannot work without the support of the designers, technical expert. And most essentially the supportive top management.

Today Industrial marketing also encompasses the internet marketing.

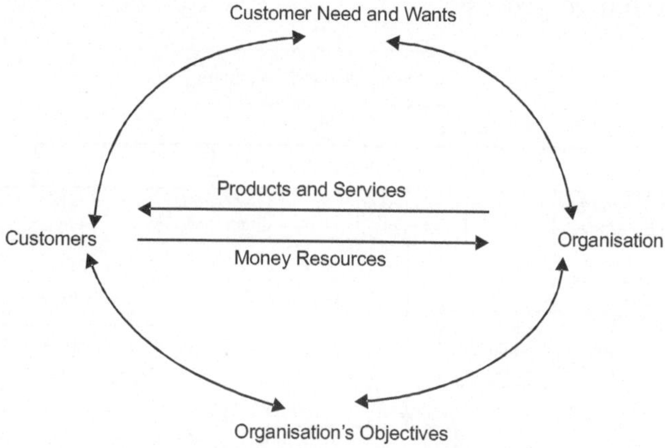

Fig. 6.2. Organisation and Customer interaction for marketing

There are online marketing websites which give a platform for buyers and sellers. We can find electric motors, polycarbonate resin tyres a whole range of other products offered by the suppliers for sale. This kind of sites, are called B2B (Business to business) websites. It eliminates the lengthy procedures of negotiations and background checks of companies etc. before the Industrial products is purchased. One such company is Alibaba. com based in China with a turnover of over $11 million.

Critical changes have occurred in Industrial markets over the past decade. Business firms are demanding higher products quality from their suppliers, faster deliver, better service and lower prices. The Industrial firms need to speed up their product development process because of shorter products life cycles. They also need to find better ways to distribute and promote their product at lower cost. The Industrial marketing concepts would help marketers to achieve their goal.[4]

The marketing process facilitates an exchange process between customers and company. What defers between the different types of organisations is not the need for an exchange process, but the nature of what is not the need for an exchange process.

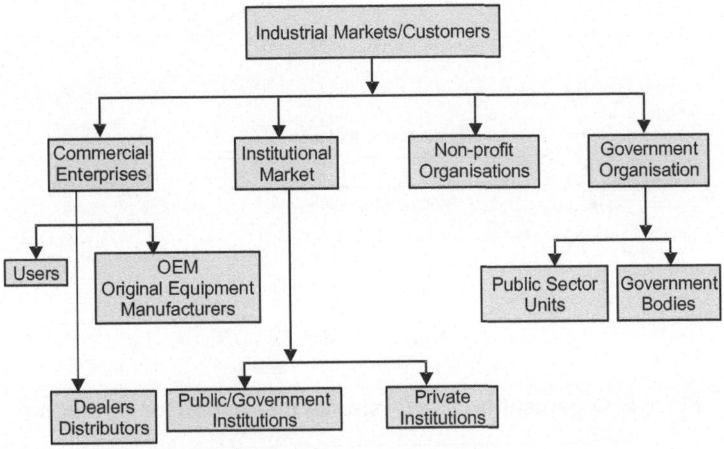

Fig. 6.3. Industrial Marketers and its Customers

Commercial Enterprises

As the term indicates the category of customers are giving large volume and profit making business, for purposes other than selling directly ultimate customers. They purchase products for different uses and it is more useful from a marketing point of view to define them in such a way as to understand their purchasing needs so that an effective marketing can be designed. This category can be further divided into (a) Users. (b) Dealers, (c) Distributors and (d) OEM

(a) Users : The particular market uses the Industrial product to facilitate its operation of business.

(b) Dealers and Distributors : Organisations which purchase the industrial goods and in turn resell them come under this category. They are members of channel through which the goods reach the customers. Even the channel members remain independent of manufacturer free to seek their own goals. Both parties agree to work together for common goals and even greater profits either would achieve independently.

(*c*) ***OEM (Original Equipment Manufacturer) :*** IQ InfoTech Limited, specialist in automotive electronics, is the OE supplier to Ashok Leyland, Best and Crompton, engineering and leading automotive companies. The products supplied are buzzers, revers beepers, head lamps, electronic flashers and dual head lamps.

Institutional Market

The institutional market consists of schools, hospitals nursing homes, prisons, and other institutions that must provide goods and services to people in their care. Many of these organisations are characterised by low budget and captive clientele. For example hospitals have to decide what quality of food to buy for the patients. The buying objectives is not profit since the food is provided to the patients as a part of the total service package.

Non-profit Organisation

Marketing is increasingly being applied outside of traditional profit marketing sector. Hospitals, charity homes, orphanages, old age homes, museums, and so on are examples of non-profit organisation, using marketing tool.

Government Organisation

In India Government organisations are major buyer of goods and services. Government organisations typically requires suppliers to submit bids and normally they award contract to the lowest bidder. In some cases the Government will make allowance for supplier of superior quality and reputation for completing contracts on time, because their spending decisions are subject to public review. Government organisations require considerable paper work from supplier. They are bound to be excessive paper work, bureaucracy, regulation, decision-making delays and frequent shifts in procurement personnel.

1. Material and parts are goods that enter the manufacturer and product completely. They fall in to two classes.

(*a*) Raw materials fall into two major classes: (1) farm product (Wheat, cotton, fruits); (2) natural products (fish, iron, ore, timber and the like) each is marketed differently. Farm products are supplied by many suppliers, who turn them over to marketing intermediaries. Natural products are of limited nature in supply. They usually have great bulk and low unit value and require substantial transportation to move them from producer to user. Price and delivery reliability are major factors influencing the selection of suppliers.

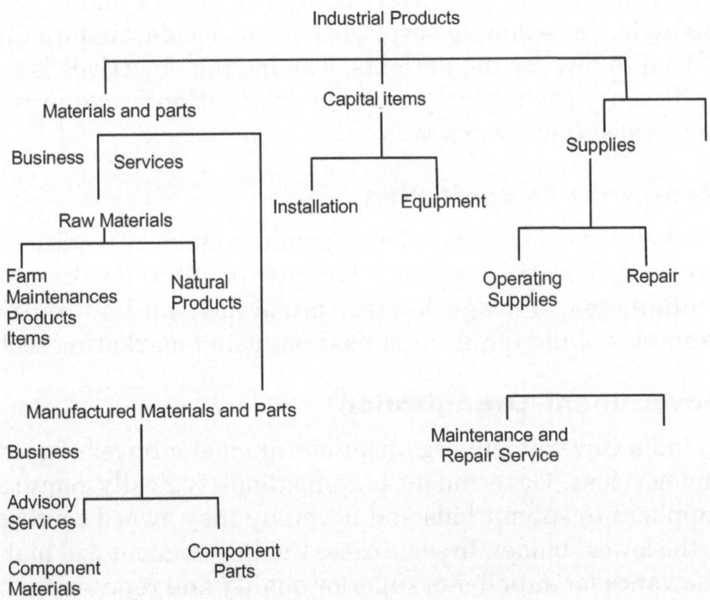

Fig. 6.4 Category of Industrial Products

(*b*) Manufactured materials and parts are divided into two categories:

- Component material (Iron, steel, yarn, cement)
- Component parts (small motor, steel castings)

Component materials are fabricated further. For example pig iron is made into steel and yarn is woven into cloth. The standardised nature of component materials usually means that price and supplier reliability are the important factors. Component parts enter the product completely with no further change in farm as when small motors are put into vacuum cleaners.

2. Capital items are long lasting goods that facilitate developing and for managing the finished product. They include

(*a*) Installations concepts of building (factories and offices) there are major purchases. They are usually bought directly from the producers, with the capital sale preceded by long negotiation period.

(*b*) Equipment companies of portable factory equipment and tools (example. Hand tools, fork lift trucks) and office equipments. (personal computers, desktops). These types of equipment do not become a part of the finished product but only aid in the operation of the business.

3. Supplies and business services are short lasting goods and services that facilitate developing and/or managing the finished product.

Supplies are two kinds: (*a*) Operating supplies (lubricants, coal, writing paper and (*b*) maintenance and repair item (paint, nails, brooms).

They are purchased with minimum effort on a strait survey basis, they are usually marketed through the intermediaries because of their low unit value and geographic destination of customers.

Business services include: (*a*) maintenance and repair service (window cleaning, carpet cleaning, computer repair (b) business advisory services (legal, management consulting, advertising).

These services are usually supplied on contract and by small products who goes by service and reputation.

The service Business as a system.

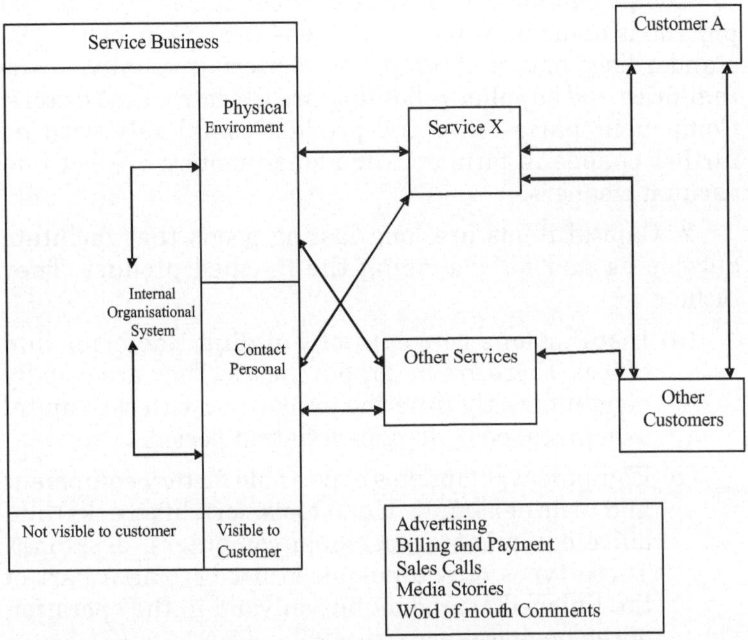

Source : Slightly modified from P Eiglier and Langeard, "A conceptual Approach to the service offering, "in proceedings of the EAARMS Annual conference, ed-it-ltartring lessen & S iteede. (Copenhagen. Copenhagen school of Business and Administration)[5]

Fig. 6.5. Service Business as a System

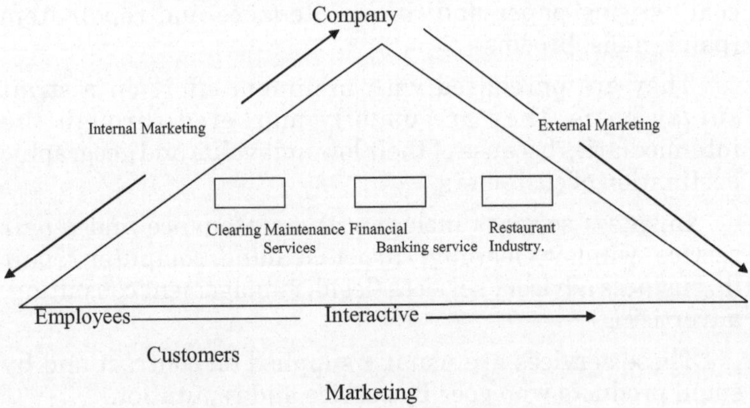

Fig. 6.6. Interactive Service Marketing

In view of this complexity, it has been argued that service marketing requires not only external marketing, but also internal and interactive marketing.

REFERENCES

1. *Marketing Management* by Philip Kotler (Eleventh Edition); Prentice Hall of India.
2. *Marketing Management* by Nand Kumari by Himalaya Publishing House.
3. *Text Book of Logistics and Supply Chain Management* by DK Agrawal–Macmillan Publication.
4. *Industrial Marketing* by Sen and Sen, Himalaya Publishing House.
5. *Marketing Management* by Philip Kotler (Eleventh Edition); Prentice Hall of India.

Financial Analysis of CONCOR

Chapter 7

INTRODUCTION

Financial analysis is the process of identifying the financial strengths and weaknesses of the firm by properly establishing relationships between the items of the balance sheet and the profit and loss account. Balance of sheet gives a summary of the firm's resources (assets) and obligations (liabilities and owners' equity) at a point of time where the profit and loss account reflects the results of the business operations by summarising revenues and expenses during a period of time. The balance sheet gives a static view of the sources and uses of finances and it does not indicate the causes of changes or the movement of finances between two periods. Similarly profit and loss account only consider revenue items and discloses net profit or net loss made during a particular period. In order to have a better understanding of the financial position of the company financial analysis of financial statement is done. The purpose of financial analysis is to diagnose the information contained in financial statements so as to judge the profitability and financial soundness of the firm. The analysis and interpretation of financial statements is essential to bring out the mystery behind the figures in financial statements.[1] There are various methods or techniques used in analysing financial statements, such as comparative statements, trend analysis, common-size statements, schedule of changes in working capital, funds flow and cash flow analysis, cost –volume – profit analysis and ratio analysis. For the financial analysis of CONCOR, ratio analysis and cash flow methods are used in order to find the financial viability of the company as both these methods found significant and suitable for financial statement analysis. For this purpose data of balance sheet and profit and loss account are taken. Time duration of the financial analysis of CONCOR in the research is taken for six years[2]. Following are the ways financial analysis and its interpretation has been done.

PROFITABILITY RATIO

Profitability indicates the efficiency with which a business is carried out. Owners are interested to know the profitability as it indicates the returns which they can get on their investments. The important profitability ratios are:

- *Overall Profitability Ratio:* Also called Return on Investment

ROI = (Operating Profit / Capital Employed) * 100

Operating Profit means 'Profit before interest and tax'

Capital Employed is the sum total of long-term funds employed in the business.

Significance : It measures the profit that a firm earns on investing a unit of capital. The business can survive only when the return on capital employed is more than the cost of capital employed.

- *Earnings Per Share:*

EPS = (Net profit after tax and Preference dividend / No. of Equity Shares)

Significance : Helps in determining the market price of the equity share of the company. A comparison of the EPS of one company with another will help in deciding if the equity share capital is being effectively used or not. It also helps in estimating the company's capacity to pay dividend to its equity shareholders.

Table 7.1. Ratio Analysis : Profitability ratios (%)

Year	2001-02	2002-03	2003-04	2004-05	2005-06	2006-07
(Non-Annualised)	12 months	12 months	12 months	12 months	12 months	12 months
PBDITA/Total income	31.8861077	31.2314598	30.9954082	32.7961459	30.3173705	31.3813694
PBDTA/Total income	31.5980095	31.0330471	30.9773258	32.7819622	30.3081388	31.3813694
PBIT/Total income	29.380776	28.3730159	27.9657859	29.5431869	26.9927471	28.4340945
PBT/Total income	29.0926778	28.1746032	27.9477035	29.5290032	26.9835154	28.4340945
PAT/Total income	18.6680136	17.7498048	20.1421385	20.9625355	21.1045151	22.4861901
Cash profit/ Total income	20.6450406	20.2465522	22.1547633	23.8251981	24.3653192	25.1337855
PBDITA /Sales	32.6788241	32.0823465	31.4199705	33.7739083	30.9162099	32.0453431
PBDTA /Sales	32.3795532	31.8765477	31.4012269	33.7593729	30.9067304	32.0453431
PBIT /Sales	30.0763335	29.1174942	28.2795638	30.4402743	27.5023699	29.008096
PBT /Sales	29.7770626	28.9116954	28.2608202	30.4257388	27.4928904	29.008096
PAT /Sales	18.9481212	18.0988239	20.1698285	21.6468182	21.4561266	22.8786188
Cash profit /Sales	21.5513891	21.0778459	23.3102351	24.7709411	25.0278201	25.9198167
PAT Net of PE&OI/ Net sales	18.9638942	18.1254857	20.1870275	21.6701706	21.4733846	22.9025975

Table 7.2. Return ratios (%)

Container Corpn. of India Ltd.	2001- 02	2002- 03	2003-04	2004-05	2005-06	2006-07
(Non-Annualised)	**12 mths**	**12 mths**	**12 mths**	**12 mths**	**12 mths**	**12 mths**
Return ratios						
On Net worth						
PBIT Net of P&E/ Avg. net worth	45.9053348	42.9207985	40.1726677	39.4876463	35.213843	37.325143
PAT Net of P&E/ Avg. net worth	28.9204084	26.6786684	28.6523449	28.0806242	27.4722752	29.4382546
PAT/Avg. net worth	29.5978597	27.1381824	29.6593041	27.8673602	27.7472143	29.8165643
Cash profit/ Avg. net worth	32.7324067	30.9555306	32.6228946	31.6729519	32.0343648	33.3272612
On Capital Employed						
PBIT Net of P&E/ Avg. capital employed	43.1442733	41.4964613	39.7499511	39.1997651	35.1156286	37.325143
PBIT/Avg. capital employed	43.780978	41.9407262	40.7463145	38.9880559	35.3898009	37.7034527
PAT Net of P&E/ Avg. capital employed	27.1809368	25.7933303	28.3508509	27.8759048	27.3956527	29.4382546
PAT/Avg. capital employed	27.8176415	26.2375952	29.3472143	27.6641957	27.669825	29.8165643

...(Contd.)

Container Corpn. of India Ltd.	**2001- 02**	**2002- 03**	**2003-04**	**2004-05**	**2005-06**	**2006-07**
On Total Assets						
PBIT Net of P&E/ Avg. total assets	34.7404478	31.9847314	30.6439105	31.156279	28.3564648	30.1054473
PBIT/Avg. total assets	35.2531324	32.3271629	31.4120239	30.9880109	28.5778635	30.4105816
PAT Net of P&E/ Avg. total assets	21.886518	19.8810384	21.8561511	22.1559866	22.1224535	23.7440972
PAT/Avg. total assets	22.3992027	20.2234699	22.6242645	21.9877185	22.3438523	24.0492315

Table 7.3. Liquidity ratios (times)

Container Corpn. of India Ltd.	2001- 02	2002- 03	2003-04	2004-05	2005-06	2006-07
(Non-Annualised)	12 mths	12 mths	12 mths	12 mths	12 mths	12 mths
Cash to current liabilities	1.95774926	1.72843917	2.12482194	2.0528579	1.84865225	2.32560023
Cash to avg. cost of sales	137.672455	127.462694	156.278525	127.827604	129.407872	166.331591
Quick ratio	2.13331688	1.88809485	2.31442308	2.26935079	2.08502901	2.55779037
Current ratio	2.22388944	1.96540523	2.48792735	2.32003958	2.41456847	2.96010155
Current ratio (incl. mktbl. securites)	2.22388944	1.96540523	2.48792735	2.32003958	2.41456847	2.96010155
Debt to equity ratio	0.08938646	0.04041725	0.01957538	0.0193965	0.03189602	0.04234114
Structure of current assets						
Inventories	1.53	2.53	2.95	3.38	4.73	4.61

...(Contd.)

Container Corpn. of India Ltd.	2001- 02	2002- 03	2003-04	2004-05	2005-06	2006-07
Sundry debtors (outstanding less than six months)	8.49	7.45	4.98	4.66	7.35	7.85
Sundry debtors (outstanding over six months)	0.56	0.89	0.8	1.07	1.17	2.05
Acccured income, lease rent and other receivables	27.08	31.87	48.26	52.23	77.8	98.24
Expenses paid in advance	11.14	11.24	36.61	2.52	109.63	174.31
Deposits	5.12	4.38	8.36	6.35	3.18	2.85
Sale of investments & other receivables	0	0	0	0	0	0
Cash & bank balance	396.64	425.71	598.98	549.85	676.34	1062.59
Structure of current assets (%)						
Inventories	0.33957741	0.52268408	0.42226707	0.55440737	0.54380317	0.34085028

...(Contd.)

Container Corpn. of India Ltd.	2001- 02	2002- 03	2003-04	2004-05	2005-06	2006-07
Sundry debtors (outstanding less than six months)	1.88432173	1.539129	0.71284408	0.76436046	0.84502184	0.58040665
Sundry debtors (outstanding over six months)	0.12428977	0.1838691	0.1145131	0.17550766	0.13451368	0.15157116
Bills receivable	0	0	0	0	0	0
Acccured income, lease rent and other receivables	6.0102983	6.5841666	6.90800303	8.56707017	8.94458496	7.26358595
Expenses paid in advance	2.47247869	2.32212214	5.24040595	0.41334514	12.6040469	12.8879852
Deposits	1.13636364	0.90488389	1.19666194	1.04156415	0.36560129	0.21072089
Sale of invest-ments and other receivables	0	0	0	0	0	0
Cash and bank balance	88.0326705	87.949343	85.7388242	90.1896139	77.7581053	78.5648799

...(Contd.)

Container Corpn. of India Ltd.	2001- 02	2002- 03	2003-04	2004-05	2005-06	2006-07
Net working capital	247.96	237.76	417.81	346.88	509.57	895.59
Net working capital (as per cost of sales method)	1145.84354	2005.8167	3672.32739	2876.66624	5083.55179	4965.76591

Table 7.4. Cash flow Statement

Container Corpn. of India Ltd.	2001- 02	2002- 03	2003-04	2004-05	2005-06	2006-07
Rs. Crore (Non-Annualised)	12 mths	12 mths	12 mths	12 mths	12 mths	12 mths
Net cash flow from operating activities (indirect method)	**226.17**	**338.01**	**462.21**	**512.6**	**548.07**	**728.73**
Net profit before tax and extra ordinary income	389.17	430.8	498.72	609.6	670.13	882.25
Adjustments for depreciation	33.47	43.94	55.28	66.62	83.26	93.58
Adjustments for interest payable	2.87	2.74	0.25	0.29	0.23	0
Adjustments for foreign exchange (gain)/loss	0.01	0.05	0	-0.01	0	0
Adjustments for add back of amortisations and others written off	0	0	0	0.08	3.83	0.12
Adjustments for add back of other provisional	0	0	0	0	0	0.13
Adjustments for (profit)/loss on sale of assets	0.05	0.09	-0.07	0.43	0.1	0.19
Adjustments for interest income	-39.49	-43.92	-35.47	-37.56	-42.68	-70.49
Adjustments for provision / liab. written back	0	0	0	0	-2.04	0

...(Contd.)

Container Corpn. of India Ltd.	**2001- 02**	**2002- 03**	**2003-04**	**2004-05**	**2005-06**	**2006-07**
Operating cash flow before working capital changes	386.08	433.7	518.71	639.45	712.83	905.78
Cash flow due to change in trade receivables	-43.35	13.5	52.76	-3.75	-26.07	-23.86
Cash flow due to change in inventories	1.04	-0.99	-0.42	-0.43	-1.35	0.12
Cash flow due to change in payables	12.51	27.56	23.3	10.83	101.15	72.33
Cash flow generated from operations	**356.28**	**473.77**	**594.35**	**646.1**	**786.56**	**954.37**
Cash (outflow) due to direct taxes paid	-129.73	-138.06	-126.02	-134.3	-238.38	-225.29
Cash flow before extraordinary items	226.55	335.71	468.33	511.8	548.18	729.08
Cash inflow/(outflow) from extraordinary items	-0.38	2.3	-6.12	0.8	-0.11	-0.35

...(Contd.)

Container Corpn. of India Ltd.	2001- 02	2002- 03	2003-04	2004-05	2005-06	2006-07
Operating cash flow before working capital changes	386.08	433.7	518.71	639.45	712.83	905.78
Cash flow due to change in trade receivables	-43.35	13.5	52.76	-3.75	-26.07	-23.86
Cash flow due to change in inventories	1.04	-0.99	-0.42	-0.43	-1.35	0.12
Cash flow due to change in payables	12.51	27.56	23.3	10.83	101.15	72.33
Cash flow generated from operations	**356.28**	**473.77**	**594.35**	**646.1**	**786.56**	**954.37**
Cash (outflow) due to direct taxes paid	-129.73	-138.06	-126.02	-134.3	-238.38	-225.29
Cash flow before extraordinary items	226.55	335.71	468.33	511.8	548.18	729.08
Cash inflow/(outflow) from extraordinary items	-0.38	2.3	-6.12	0.8	-0.11	-0.35

...(Contd.)

Container Corpn. of India Ltd.	2001- 02	2002- 03	2003-04	2004-05	2005-06	2006-07
Net cash inflow/(outflow) from investment activities	**-100.25**	**-200.9**	**-205.67**	**-424.13**	**-273.66**	**-201.67**
Cash (outflow) due to purchase of fixed assets	-147.81	-230	-216.8	-341.83	-259.86	-233.57
Cash inflow due to sale of fixed assets	0.03	0.07	0.51	0.67	0.05	0.01
Cash inflow/(outflow) due to decrease/(increase) in capital wip	0	0	-21.98	-40.03	-10.15	-37.29
Cash inflow /(outflow) due to acquisition/ merger/ hiving off of cos./ units	27.73	-14.89	0	0	0	0
Cash (outflow) due to purchase of investments	-0.66	0	-2.79	-80.55	-45.51	-2.32
Cash inflow due to sale of investments	0	0	0	0	0.12	0
Cash inflow/(outflow) due to loans to subs./group cos.	0	0	-0.08	0.05	-0.99	1.01
Cash inflow due to interest received	20.46	43.92	35.47	37.56	42.68	70.49

...(Contd.)

Container Corpn. of India Ltd.	2001- 02	2002- 03	2003-04	2004-05	2005-06	2006-07
Net cash inflow/ (outflow) from financing activities	**-49.08**	**-108.05**	**-83.28**	**-137.6**	**-147.92**	**-140.81**
Cash inflow due to proceeds from total borrowings	30.46	0	0	0	0	0
Cash inflow due to proceeds from long term borrowings	30.46	0	0	0	0	0
Cash (outflow) due to repayment of total borrowings	-29.04	-40.28	-2.38	-1.39	-10.6	0
Cash (outflow) due to repayment of long term liabilities	-29.04	-40.28	-2.38	-1.39	-10.6	0
Cash (outflow) due to interest paid	-2.49	-2.74	-0.25	-0.29	-0.23	0
Cash (outflow) due to dividend paid	-48	-64.98	-80.64	-135.93	-137.09	-140.81
Cash inflow/(outflow) due to other cash receipts/payables from financing activities	-0.01	-0.05	-0.01	0.01	0	0
Net cash inflow/(outflow) due to net increase/(decrease) in cash & cash equivalents	76.84	29.06	173.26	-49.13	126.49	386.25
Cash flow — opening balance	293.18	396.65	425.72	598.98	549.85	676.34
Cash flow — closing balance	370.02	425.71	598.98	549.85	676.34	1062.59

- *Price Earning Ratio :* This ratio indicates the no. of times the earning per share is covered by its market price.

PER = (Mkt. price per equity share / Earning per share)

Significance : Helps the investor in determining whether or not to buy the shares of a company at a particular price.

- *Gross Profit Ratio:*

  Gross profit ratio = (Gross Profit / Net Sales) * 100

Significance : Indicates the degree to which the selling price of goods per unit may decline without resulting in losses from operations to the firm. It also helps in ascertaining whether the average percentage of mark-up on the goods is maintained.

Gross profits should be adequate to cover operating expenses and to provide for fixed charges, dividends and building up of reserves.

- *Net Profit Ratio :*

  Net Profit Ratio = (Net Operating Profit / Net Sales) * 100

Significance : An increase in this ratio over the previous period indicates improvement in the operational efficiency of the business provided the gross profit ratio is constant.

- ***Operating Ratio :*** This ratio is the complementary of the net profit ratio. In case the net profit ratio is 20 per cent, the operating ratio is 80 per cent.

Operating Ratio = (Operating Costs / Net Sales) * 100

Operating costs include the cost of direct materials, direct labour and other overheads *viz.* factory, office or selling.

Significance : It tests the operational efficiency with which the business is being carried. The ratio should be low enough to leave a portion of sales to give a fair return to the investors. Incase of an increase in the ratio overtime, the reason should be found out and management be advised to check the same.

- *Fixed Charges Cover:* Also known as the Debt Service Ratio/ Interest Coverage Ratio, it indicates whether the business would earn sufficient profits to pay periodically the interest charges.

Debt Service Ratio=(Income before Int and Tax / Interest charges)

The standard for this ratio for an industrial company is that interest charges should be covered six to seven times.

- *Debt Service Coverage Ratio:* The interest coverage ratio does not tell anything about the ability of the company to make principal payment on time. This insight is provided by

Debt Service Coverage = (Net Profit before Interest and Tax) /
Ratio (Interest + Principal payment installment)

The principal instalment is adjusted for tax effects since such payments is not deductible from net profit for tax purposes.

- *Payout Ratio:* Indicates the proportion of earnings per share that has been used for paying dividends.

  Payout Ratio = Dividend per equity share/ Earnings per equity share

A complementary to this ratio is the Retained earning Ratio = Retained Earning per equity share/ Earning per equity share.

Significance: The payout and retained earning ratios are indicators of the amount of earnings that have been ploughed back in the business. Lower the payout ratio, higher will be the earnings ploughed back in the business and vice versa.

- *Dividend Yield Ratio:* Useful for investors interested only in dividend income;

  DYR = Dividend per share/ Mkt price per share

TURNOVER RATIOS

Turnover Ratios or activity ratios indicate the efficiency with which capital employed is rotated in the business.

- *Fixed Assets Turnover Ratio:* Indicates the extent to which investments in fixed assets contributed towards sales. It is calculated as : Net Sales / Fixed Assets
- *Working Capital Turnover Ratio:* Indicates whether or not working capital has been effectively utilised in making sales.
- *It is calculated as:* Net Sales / Working Capital.

It can take the following different forms:

1. Debtor's Turnover Ratio = Credit Sales / Avg. Accts receivable Higher the ratio, better it is, since it would indicate that debts are being collected more promptly.
2. *Debt Collection Period Ratio:* Indicates the extent to which debt is collected on time. An increase in the period will result in greater blockage of funds in debtors. The ratio may be calculated as under.
   - Months (or days) in a year/ Debtor's Turnover
   - Accounts Receivable/ Avg. Monthly or daily credit sales
3. *Creditor's Turnover Ratio :* Indicates the speed with which payments for credit purchases are made to creditors. It is calculated as : Credit Purchases / Avg. Accts. Payable
4. *Average Age of Payables :* Indicates the average credit period enjoyed from creditors. It may be calculated as :
   - Months (or days) in a year / Creditor's Turnover
   - Avg Accts payable/ Avg Monthly (or daily) Credit Purchases
5. *Stock Turnover Ratio:* Indicates whether investment in inventory is efficiently used or not. It is measured as :

   Cost of goods sold during the year / Avg. Inventory

A high ratio indicates brisk sales. A low ratio results in blocking of funds in inventory which may ultimately result in heavy losses due to inventory becoming obsolete or deteriorating in quality.

Financial Ratios indicate the financial soundness of the company. Some important Financial Ratios are :

- Fixed Asset Ratio : Fixed Assets / Long-term funds

RATIO ANALYSIS AND INTERPRETATION

PBDITA = Profit Before Depreciation Interest Tax and Amortisation

PBDTA = Profit Before Depreciation Tax and Amortisation

PBIT = Profit Before Interest and Tax

PBT = Profit Before Tax

PAT = Profit After Tax

From the computation of various profitability it is clear that the profitability of the company has been almost same in last year. These has been slight decrees in the

$$= \frac{\text{PBDITA}}{\text{Total Income Ratio}}$$

as it was 31-89 per cent in 2001-02 which came down to 31.38 per cent. There has been decline of 0.5 per cent in this ratio.The same condition is with other profitability ratio except net profit to sales ratio.PAT/Sales ratio was 18.95 per cent on 31st March 2002 which went up to 22.88 per cent on 21st March 2007.

There has been another important fact which has been revealed from profitability ratio is that the profitability has not been moving in one direction always. There has been slight decrease and increase in each year profitability ratio as compared to previous one. If we take PBIT/Total Income as a criterion to measure profitability of the company, we find that first three year of study PBIT /Total income has been decreasing as it was 29.38 per cent on 31st March 2002 which declined to 28.37 per cent in March 2003, again declined to 27.97 per cent in March 2004.

In Financial Year 2004-05 this ratio improved went up to 29.54 per cent but in the next year it came down drastically to 26.99 per cent Again in 2006-07, some improvement were seen in this ratio as it stood up 28.43 per cent. The same condition is with PBIT/sales ratio and PBT/Sales ratio.

As per the cash profit ratio is concern, it gives us rosy picture of the profitability of the company. As cash profit to total income was 20.64 per cent in March 2002 which increased up to the 25.13 per cent in March 2007. While Cash profit/Sales increased from 21.55 per cent to 25.92 per cent during the same period.

Finally it can be inferred that keeping the nature of company in mind (monopoly),the company has been maintaining consistency in its profitability and no speculation or abnormality is seen in the earning capacity of the company.

(*i*) Return on Networth

(*ii*) Return on Capital employed

(*iii*) Return on Total Assets

(*i*) *Return on Net worth:* As per the PBIT/Average network ratio is concerned, it shows the conservative financial policy of the company as there is continuous decrease in ratio. The return on network which was 45.91 per cent in March 2002 came down by 9 per cent and stood at 37.32 per cent in March 2007. This shows that company has failed to provide consistent return to its shareholders as company is not willing to face any kind of financing risk remain adhered with conservative financing policy. That is why almost consistent profitability ratio, the return on networth has declined significantly.

Though the profit after tax (PAT/Average Network) shows just opposite result, as there has been 0.22 per cent increase in this ratio. Though it is nominal to make any inference.

(*ii*) Return on Capital Employed : PBIT/Average capital employed (Return on capital Employed). reduced from

43 per cent to 37 per cent same explanation as has been explained in Return on Networth.

Return on Capital employed of the company has continuously decreased.

Reasons

1. Issue of extra shares
2. Mobilisation of additional capital which has been failed to generate proportionate return.

The basic reason behind this shortfall is inappropriate use of borrowed fund during the course of study the company has not been using its retained earnings and additional capital for generating adequate profit.

(*iii*) ***Return on Total Asset :*** Return on total asset has been declined by the five basis point as it decreased from 35.255 per cent to 30.41 per cent during the course of study. The reason is same as above that is lackness in proper allocation of company's financial resources.

Short-term Liquidity Position

Short term liquidity position indicates the strength of company to discharge its short term financial obligation.. Generally obligation falling within an operating cycle.The short-term payment capacity can be judged by computing mainly by current ratio and liquid ratio. Its results are as follows:

(1) ***Current Ratio :*** This ratio is numerical relationship between current assets and current liabilities of the company and expressed in times. As per the result of the ratio is concerned, it was found that in financial year 2002-03 the current ratio was below standard. As ideal current ratio is 2:1 in 2002-03 current ratio was 1.9654 :1.In rest of the year, the ratio has been more than standard and in last three years, it has increasing trend.

In 2004-05, the ratio was 2.3:1.where in 2005-06 it increased to 2.4:1. Further it was all time high in financial year 2006-07 with 2.9:1. Over all picture shows that the company is quite capable to meet its short terms financial obligations.

(2) ***Liquid Ratio :*** Liquid /Quick Ratio

This ratio describes the immediate payment capacity of the company. The standard ratio is 1:1.

In case of Container Corporation India (CONCOR), the liquid ratio is very good throughout the study period. It means that company has sufficient cash and marketable securities to discharge any financial obligations arising immediately. The quick ratio was 2.1: in 2001-02, which increased up to 2.6:1 in 2006-07. Though the ratio was maintained all-time in march 2003.

The Test of Long-term Solvency Position of Company

To test long-term payment capacity of the company, average ratio or debt equity are analysed. This ratio establishes mathematical relationship between long term liabilities (debt fund)and shareholders fund (equity/own fund). Higher the ratio, poor will be the payment capacity and the company will be working on higher risk and vice versa. In case of this company long-term solvency position is good and company is unwilling to take financial risk, therefore it is not trading on equity.

Inspite of fact that there has been good atmosphere, to raise debt fund from the market, the company adhered with the share capital only. The debt equity ratio has been found much below standard. In 2001-02 the ratio was 0.089:1, on March 31st 2003 it came down to 0.04:1. Again it come down to 0.0196:1 on 31st March 2004-05. It was 0.0412:1 on 31st March 2007.

All these results indicate that company keeping safe hands while meeting its long-term financial requirement.This company is fundamentally quite strong. Investor can invest in the company for the consistent results. The company is suitable for the risk averter and risk neutral class investor.

ANALYSIS OF CASH FLOW STATEMENT OF CONTAINER CORPORATION OF INDIA LTD

Cash flow basically deals with flow of cash and cash equivalent from three main activities *i.e.* operating activities, investing activities and financing activities during particular period. Here the analysis of these three has been done separately as follows.

I. Cash from Operating Activities

This activity shows the competency of the firm in generating cash profit from its main activity or day to day activities. From the analysis of cash from operating activity one can also assess the firm's tax liability and depreciation charged during the year.

As per the analysis of operating activities of the company is concerned the net profit before tax, extra ordinary income was Rs. 389.17 crores in March 2002 which has been continuously increasing up to the March 2007 and reach at 882.25 crores. This has been increased by 126.74 per cent. But cash from operation during the same period reached to Rs. 728.73 crores, in March 2007 from 226.17 crores in March 02. In percentage it has increased by 222.21 per cent Means that proportionate in crease in cash from operating activity its has been greater than percentage increase in net profit before tax and extra ordinary income it mainly due to proportionately less increase in non-operating items during the course of study.

The adjustment of depreciation to operating cash has been 33.47 crores in March 2002 that goes up to the 93.58 crores while interest income received, deducted during the period has been increased from Rs. 39.49 crores to Rs. 70.49 crore.

The operating cash flow before working capital changes stand at very good position as it was Rs. 386.08 crores in March 2002, Rs. 433.7 crores in March 03, Rs. 518.7 crores in March 2004, 639.45 crores in March 2005, Rs. 712.83

crores in 2006 and Rs. 905.78 crores in March 2007, there fore increase by 134.64 per cent over the period can be regarded as considerable growth.

The tax paid during the period has been increased from Rs. 129.73 crores to 225.29 crores which is mainly because of increase in EBIT of the company that is good sign for the company and express sound profitability position of the company.

II. Analysis of Cash Flow from Investing Activities

It shows the capacity of a firm to spend fund on innovation, modernisation and expansion through buying more plant and machinery and spending on gross block. The company has been succeeded in this direction as company has invested Rs. 100.25 crores during 2001-02. 200.9 crores in 2002-03 and Rs. 424.13 crores in 2004-05, though flow on investing activities has been considerably declined in F.Y 2006-07, as it came down to Rs. 201.67 crores only.

III. Cash from Financing Activities

This analysis shows the sources of fund from where company has catered its financial need and cost of capital paid by company to the supplier of funds. The company has not issued a single share during the period and only in 2001-02 the long-term borrowing was made of Rs. 30.46 crores, though the repayment of existing loan has been made during this year which resulted net outflow of cash Rs. 49.08 crores in this year. Rest of the years only cash out flow can be seen, basically on interest and dividend payment and repayment of borrowing these resulted total out flow of cash Rs. 140.81 crores in 2006-07.

REFERENCES

1. *Financial Management* by I.M. Pandey, Vikas Publishing, New Delhi.
2. *Annual Financial Report of Container Corporation of India,* 2002-07.

Human Resource Management Practices in CONCOR

Chapter 8

INTRODUCTION

Human Resource at the organisational level includes all the component resources of all employees from rank and file to top management level, all the employees like managing director, board of directors, persons who work on honorary basis, experts drawn from various organisation, and there people (particularly family members) influencing the Human Resources of the former group. In short it includes the resources of all the people who contribute their services to the attainment of organisational goal and often who contribute their service is order to create trundles in the attainment of organisational goals.

Meaning of Human Resource Management

Different terms are used to denote Human Resource Management. They are labour management labour administration, labour-management relation, employer-employee relation, industrial relations, personnel administration, personnel management, human capital management, human asset management human resource management and the like. Through these terms can be differentiated widely, the basic nature of distortions lies in the scope or coverage and evolutionary stage. In simple sense. Human Resource Management means employing people, developing their resource, utilising, maintaining and comporting their services in tune with the goal and organisational requirements.[1]

Human Resource Management is concerned with employees both as individuals and as group in attaining goals. It is also concerned with behaviour, emotional and social aspects of personnel. It is conserved with the development of human resources, *i.e.* knowledge, capability, skill, potentialities and attaining and achieving employee-goals including job-satisfaction. Human Resource Management covers all levels (low, middle and top) and categories unsuited, skilled, technical, professional, clerical and managerial of employees. It covers both organised and unorganised employees. It applies to the employees in all types of organisations in world (industry, trade, service, commerce, economic, social, religions, political and government departments). Thus it is common in all types of organisations.[2]

PUBLIC SECTOR IN INDIAN ECONOMY

State intervention in the economic or business activities is no longer an economic anathema or the political taboo of the past. It is now regarded as an inescapable part of the obligation of the present day governments to redress economic imbalances, to safeguard the interests and welfare of the community as a whole, to plan for overall rapid, progress and prosperity and to undertake and execute schemes and projects right to the needs of the notions. Theme is very little don't that the future of the developing camp only and its ability to met national aspirations of removal of poverty and faster improvement in living standard would largely depend upon the role assigned to the public enterprises.

In India, the public sector came into being with the adoption of Industrial Policy Resolution, 1948, which laid down that industries of basic and strategic importance and public utility should be in the public sector.[3]

Evolution of the Public Sector in India

Prior to 1947, there was virtually no 'public sector' in the Indian Economy. The only instances worthy to mention were the Railway, the posts and the telegraphs, the port trusts the ordinance and Aircraft factories and a few state managed undertakings.

However, in the post independence period, the expansion of public sector has undertaken as an integral part of the 1956 industrial policy. The Industrial policy resolution 1956 gave the public sector a strategic role in the Indian economy. For are thing, at the time of independence, the country was backward and underdeveloped, basically an agrarian economy with a weak industrial base, heavy unemployment, low level of savings and investment and near absence of infrastructural facilities, Indian economy needed a big push. This push could not come from the Indian private sector, which was starved of funds and of managerial ability and was incapable of undertaking risks involved in long gestation investments. In other words the public sector was though of as the engine for economic growth.

Born as the outcome of the country with a view to give added impetus to economic growth as well as to achieve certain socio-economic goals as enunciated in the industrial policy resolutions of the governments, there enterprises to day cover a side spectrum of activities in basic and strategic industries like steel, coal minerals and metals, petroleum, heavy engineering chemicals, fertilisers and pharmacy etc on the one hand, and consumer goods, trading and marketing activities, transportation services, travel service, financial services, development of small industries etc, on the other while some of these enterprises operate under monopoly conditions, there are other working under competitive conditions.

RECRUITMENT POLICY OF CONCOR

The major highlights of the policy are:

1. Unskilled workers should be drawn from the locality where the project is situated.
2. All efforts should be made to recruit persons, displaced from the area acquired for the project specially the SC and the STs.
3. Next preference is to be given to those, who even if come from a distance have been refreshed by other P's.
4. Skilled workers, clerks and other non-technical staffs may be recruited locally presided they fulfill the basic qualification.
5. Middle level Technical and Non-technical posts, having higher starting salaries equal to class I Junior scale of the Government of India are to he filled by the principal criteria.
6. Higher Non-technical posts should be filled from the candidates available in the industrial management pull failing which the post should be advertised on all India basis.
7. Higher Technical posts may be filled from persons recruited either by advertisement an all India basis or by personal contact.
8. Vacancies for unskilled labour clerk and other employees of low grades etc. should be communicated to the employment exchange for the project.
9. All application along with the list sent by the employment exchange be screened and appointments made by the selection committee of the unit which will have representatives or nominees from the state government.
10. For the higher and medium level posts at least one representative of the state govt-preferably a state

Government official who is on the Board of Directors should be included in the selection committee.

Conditions for Recruitment in CONCOR

Following are the conditions in CONCOR-

1. A candidate for the appointment to CONCOR must be either

(*a*) A citizen of India or

(*b*) A subject of Nepal or

(*c*) A Subject of Bhutan or

(*d*) A persons of Indian origin who has migrated from Pakistan, Burna, Sri Lanka, East African Countries of Kenya, Uganda and united Republic of Tanzania or from Zamtia, Ethiopia and Viethan with the intention of permanently setting is India.

Provided that a candidate belonging to categories (b), (c), (d) and

(*e*) above shall be persons in whose favour a certificate of eligibility has been issued by the Government of India.

2. A candidate in whose case a certificate of eligibility is necessary may be admitted to the examination but the offer of appointment will be given any after the Government of India has inset the necessary eligibility certificate to him.

3. No male candidate who has more than one wife living shall not be eligible for appointment to a CONCOR service unless the competent authority exempts the candidate from the operation of this rule.

4. All new entrant to service are required to take oath of allegiance before the head of department/office or gazetted CONCOR servant nominated by him.

5. The recruitment is subject to the reservation of vacancies in favour of SC/ST candidates as laid down by Government of India from time to time.

6. Ordinary a CONCOR servant is employed throughout his services on the railway or railway establishment to which he is posted on first appointment and has no claim as a matter of right for transfer to another railway or another establishment.

7. Two or move CONCOR servant cannot be appointed substantively to the same, permanent post at the save time. It has been observed that all the above conditions strictly followed in CONCOR.

Fixing Cadres in CONCOR/Railway

The no of permanent working posts that is posts required for ordinary duty in CONCOR shall first be determined for each service or department.

(*i*) Senior Administrative Grade I.

(*ii*) Senior Administrative Grade II

(*iii*) Administrative Grade.

(*iv*) Junior administrative Grade.

(*v*) Senior Grade.

(*vi*) Junior Scale/Group.

(*i*) General working post that is posts required for general purpose of CONCOR, which may be filled by gazette Railway officers of any services, may be determined and derided in the same manner

(*ii*) The no of post to be allotted to the junior scale shall be calculated with reference to the total no of administrative grade and senior scale posts. Continuous flow of preventions take place from lower to higher grade after a given period of service and for this purpose all the administrative post including the general administrative post shall be taken into account.

(*iii*) The rest of post included in (*i*), (*vi*) above shall be allotted to Groups B.

2. Posts required for meeting deportation leave and training requirement will be provided in Junior scale based

on requirement from time to time. These posts shall be intended ordinarily to provide for the deputation/training of and or grant of leaves to a number of department without security of making and officiating appointment to the junior scale on to a group 'B' post in the chain of vacancies consequent up not the deputation training of and/or grant of leave to the member in question.

Classification of the CONCOR Employees

As per the recommendation of fifth pay commission, the CONCOR employees have been reclassified w.e.f. 1/4/96 into following group.

Existing	Revised	Classification
Class I	Group A	Gazetted
Class II	Group B	Gazetted
Class III	Groups C	Non-Gazetted
Class IV	Group D	Non-Gazetted

1. ***Group A :*** All posts carrying a pay or a scale of pay with a maximum of not less than Rs 8000-13,500 are placed in group 'A' service the following grade ranging from Rs. 8000 + 13,500 to 24050-20000 (as per revised scale) are available to the CONCOR employees under Group 'A' service.

Table 8.1. Pay Scale of Group 'A'

Pay Scale	Major Design Alive
8000-13,500 (Junior Scale)	Assistant Electrical Engineer Assistance Marketing Manager Assistance per social officer
10,000-15,200 (Senior Grade)	Senior Marketing Manager Senior Electrical Engineer
Scale of pay 12000-16,500 (Junior Administrative Grade)	Major Designation deputy chief engineer deputy chief vigilance officer

...*(Contd.)*

Pay Scale	Major Design Alive
14,300-18,3000 (Senior Grade)	Deputy Chief Personnel Engineer, Deputy Chief Marketing Manager Deputy Financial Advisor.
18400-22400 (Senior Administrative Grade)	Chief Electrical Engineer, Chief Mechanical Engineer (Production), Financial Advisor, Chief Accounts Officer
22,400-24,500 (Higher Administrative Grade)	Controllers of Stores Chief Mechanical Engineer
24050-26,00	General Manager

Group 'B'

All posts carrying a pay or a scale of pay with a minimum of not less than Rs. 7500-12000 (in the revised scale) but less than Rs. 13,500 are placed is group 'B' gazetted service. CONCOR has got the following salary grade.

Table 8.2 Pay Scale of Group 'B' Officers

Revised Pay Scale of pay	Major Design Alive
7500-12,000	Assistant Engineers Audit Officers Assistant Work Manager Assistant Personnel Officer
8000-13,500	Assistant Financial Advisor, Assistant Marketing Manager Assistant Electrical Engineer

Group 'C'

Salary grade with a minimum pay of 2750-4400 are in group 'C' non-gajetted service. The following technical and non-technical categories of employees of CONCOR, and their respective grades are placed in groups 'C'.

Table 8.3. Pay Scale of Group 'C' Officers

Revised Pay Scale	Major Design Alive
2750-4400	Record Shorter Railway Operator
3050-4510	Dealing Clerk
4000-6000	Skill Grade II
4500-7000	Senior Clerk I
5500-9000	Section Officer
6500-10500	Assistant Account Officer Assistant Shop Superintendents.
7450-11500	Shop Superintendents Accounts Officer
7500-12000	Applicable only to Schools
8000-13500	Vice Principal/Head of the Department

Group 'D'

Recruitment of all the post in group 'D' is done by the CONCOR except for the post of Junior Clerk, Typist, Gr.-III, Staff Elurse, Pharmacists and save post of reserved categories of which recruitment is done all post carrying a pay or a scale of pay the minimum which is Rs. 2550-3200 are placed is group 'D'. The following are the categories of employees placed in these respective salary grades.

Table 8.4. Pay Scale of Group 'D' Officers

Revised Pay Scale	Major Design Alive
2550-3200	Peons, attendants, unskilled worker
2610-3740	Dafataries/Point Man
2650-4000	Jamedar/Semi-skilled workers/Khalasi

Job Description and Specification

In the observe of proper system of job analysis and job evaluation, job are not property studies before job specification are issued. Job analysis that is job description and job specification has been done at the Railway Board level except for save categories of group 'D' post of which job analysis has been done at the unit level.

Normally job specification comes minimum and maximum age limits, qualification relaxation and resonations for SC/ ST candidates and Ex-Serviceman scale of pay and important condition of service like leave, Pension, P.F. of benefits etc. No CONCOR servant his appointed and retained in service beyond the age of 58 years. However a servant or groups 'D' workers retire at the age of '60' years. A candidate is cratered for appointment only if his age according to matriculation/ School leaving certificates municipal birth certificates issued by the conserved is 18 years and above, but below the upper age limits laid down in specification.

MONETARY COMPENSATION IN CONCOR

CONCOR is supposed to be the model employer and where employees have got high expectations from the management and the Government to look after their interests, well have no doubt spend a huge sum on social overheads, in order to provide basic amenities of life to its employees. But there is a general complaint of the employees that "public sector believes in the philosophy of getting the best man for the second best price". In a mixed economy with much competitive demand for talent, the public enterprise wages should not be kept too low as compared to those offered in the private sector, otherwise it would be difficult for Public Enterprises to attract and retain talent. A Public Enterprises Manager being more akin to a private enterprise in terms of work and responsibility usually considers the managerial and technical personnel in private enterprises as his reference group. Thus if the total pay package of both are substantially different, public enterprises executives are likely to have a feeling of inequity and moreover if there is flight of talent from public enterprises to private sector it will not be unusual. The government should therefore take every step to ensure that flight of talent is checked and that the wages and salaries of the two sectors should be kept at par through appropriate measures.

The salient features of the compensation plan in CONCOR is as follows:

(*a*) A wage and salary structure having two components namely "Basic Wage and Salary" and "Dearness Allowance" in all the units and some special pay allowance in few units;

(*b*) Inter unit disparities in the existing wage and salary structures including fringe benefits;

(*c*) Co-existence of times and piece rate system of wage payments in the same unit;

(*d*) An annual minimum bonus (per the provisions of Payment of Bonus Act 1965 amended up to date) unrelated to profits and up to 20 per cent if there are reasonable profits at the unit level;

(*e*) Existence of a variety incentive schemes under different names and with different objectives both within the unit and in different units; and

(*f*) Provision of periodic wage revision (usually four years) namely on the basis of collective bargaining and more or less unrelated to profits, production and productivity. In some organisations wages are revised and restructured even at shorter intervals and in some others at longer interval say around five years.

Wages and Salaries

Wages and salaries of the CONCOR employees are fixed on the recommendation of Central Pay Commission. The different units of Indian Railway have no power to revise/

fix the scale of pay. However demands for the revision of the pay scale or the introduction of the new scales of pay may be presented by the employees of Indian Railways through their federation before Railway Boards which may either on representation or of its own accord may effect any changes with the approval of the President of India. Up to 31st March 2005. Five Pay Commissions had been appointed to recommend the pay scales for the Central Government Employees including Indian Railway.

The first pay structure was introduced by Government of India in 1931. There after the pay structure have been revised from time to time *viz*:

(*i*) 1931 – called as 31 scales of pay

(*ii*) 1934 - 34 scales of pay

(*iii*) 1947 – Prescribed scales of pay (1st Central Pay Commission

(*iv*) 1-7-59 Authorised Scales of Pay (2nd Central Pay Commission)

(*v*) 1-1-73 Revised Scales of Pay (3rd Central Pay Commission)

(*vi*) 1-1-86 Revised Pay Scale (4th Central Pay Commission)

(*vii*) 1-1-96 RSRP (5th Central Pay Commission)

Every Pay Commission has reduced the number of scale and initially what started with 153 scales has been reduced to 25 scales. In the Fourth Pay Commission it was 33 scales, which means the Fifth Pay Commission has reduced nine more scale as far as Indian Railways is concerned. The minimum basic pay as per the Fifth Central Pay Commission is Rs. 2550 and the maximum is 26000/-.

(1) *Basic Wage and Salary Grades :* The establish-ment of satisfactory relationship among emoluments of different categories of job in an organisation is necessary in order to avoid the dissatisfaction that would otherwise, develop among employees over inequalities of wages between similar jobs[8]. The gap between the highest and lowest pay is to be minimised as the policy of Government to minimise the income inequality. But at the same time the wage structure should be such as to attract and maintain the efficient personnel and at the same time provides an incentive to exploit their potentialities for the organisational success.

In the CONCOR wage and salary grades have been classified according to following categories of personnel.

A. Gazetted Personnel Grade

B. Non-Gazatted Personnel Grade

Table 8.5 Gazetted Personnel Grade/ Executive Grade

Revised Scale of Pay	Major Designation
7500-12000	Audit Officer/ Assistant Works Manager
8000-13500	Assistant Marketing Manager Assistant Electrical Engineer
10000-15200	Senior Marketing Manager
12000-165000	Deputy Chief Engineer/ Deputy Chief Vigilance Officer
14300-18300	Deputy Chief Personal Officer/ Deputy Financial Advisor/ Deputy Chief Marketing Manager
18400-22400	Chief Electrical Engineer/ Financial Advisor, Chief Accounts Officer/ Chief Mechanical Engineer (Production)
22400-24500	Controller of Stores/ Chief Mechanical Engineer
24050-26000	General Manager

***(b)* Non-Gazetted Personnel Grade** : All personnel on the group 'C' and 'D' services have been placed in the Non-Gazetted Personal Grade. Under this grade comes the unskilled, skilled, highly skilled Grade II and skilled Grade

I employees. The ministerial and electrical employees of the CONCOR also come under this category. There are in all twelve grades under the Non-Gazetted Personal Grade. The following table presents a complete view of this grade together with major designation.

Table 8.6 Non-gazetted Personnel grade

Revised Scale of Pay	Major Designation
2550-3200	Unskilled Workers
2610-3740	Daftarees / Point Men
2650-4000	Jamedar/ Semi skilled Workers.
2750-4400	Record Shorter/ Railway Operator
3050-4510	Dealing Clerk
4000-6000	Skilled Grade II
4500-7000	Senior Clerk I
5550-9000	Selection Officer
6500-10500	Assistant Accounts Officer/ Assistant Shop Superintendents
7450-11500	Shop Superintendents/ Accounts Officer
7500-12000 8000-13500	Applicable Only to SchoolsVice Principal/ Head of Departments

Table 8.7 Powers and Duties of Officers of CONCOR

S.No.	Name	Designation & Address	Duties
1.	Sh. Shri Prakash	Chairman (Non-Executive), Member Traffic, Railway Board	Non-Executive Chairman (Govt. Nominee) Chairing the Board Meetings.
2.	Sh. Rakesh Mehrotra	Managing Director	Functional Head of CONCOR and Overall incharge of entire business of CONCOR
3.	Sh. Yash Vardhan	Director (Intl. Marketing & Ops.)	Incharge of International Business

...(Contd.)

S.No.	Name	Designation & Address	Duties
			operations of CONCOR.
4.	Sh. Suresh Kumar	Director (Finance)	Incharge of all Financial/ Accounting matters.
5.	Sh. Anil Gupta	Director (Domestic)	Incharge of Domestic marketing business.
6.	Sh. Harpreet Singh	Director (Projects & Services)	Incharge of Projects, Planning & Development.
7.	Sh. K B Agrawal	Chief Vigilance Officer Corporate Office, New Delhi	Incharge of all Vigilance related matters.
8.	Ms. P Alli Rani	Executive Director (Finance) & Chief Public Relations Officer/ Corporate Office/ New Delhi	Incharge of Finance & Accounts department and Public Relations including investor relations.
9.	Capt. P.K. Kaul	Executive Director (CR & BD) Corporate Office/ New Delhi	Incharge of all matters relating to customer relations & business development
10.	Sh. Ravi Khandelwal	Executive Director (A/cs & CS)/ Corporate Office/ New Delhi	Company Secretary.
11.	Sh. Anurag Mathur	Executive Director (MIS)/ Corporate Office/ New Delhi	Incharge of procurement & maintenance of IT hardware & software.
12.	Sh. P.K. Agrawal	Chief General Manager/ Western Region, Mumbai	Overall Incharge of all matters relating to the Western Region
13.	Sh. D K Tripati	Chief General Manager/ Central Region/ Nagpur	Overall incharge of all matters relating to the Central Region.
14.	Sh. Ajoy Kumar Behra	Chief General Manager/ Eastern Region/ Kolkata	Overall incharge of all matters relating to the Eastern Region

...(Contd.)

S.No.	Name	Designation & Address	Duties
15.	Sh. Ajay Anand	Chief General Manager/Northern Region/ Tughlakabad	Overall incharge of all matters relating to Northern Region
16.	Sh. Sushil Kumar	Chief General Manager/ North Central Region/ Noida	Overall incharge of all matters relating to North Central Region
17.	Sh. G John Prasad	Chief General Manager/ Southern Region/ Chennai	Overall incharge of all matters relating to the Southern Region
18.	Sh. Shahnawaz Ali	Chief General Manager/ South Central Region/ Hyderabad	Overall incharge of all the matters relating to the South Central Region
19.	Sh. Amit Kumar Singh	Chief General Manager/ North West Region/ Ahemdabad	Overall incharge of all the matters relating to the North West Region.
20.	Sh. Mukul Jain	Group General Manager (Air Cargo)/ Corporate Office/ New Delhi	Incharge of marketing & business in Air Cargo segment.
21.	Ms. Padmakshi Raheja	Group General Manager (Business Research)/ Corporate Office/ New Delhi	Incharge of Business Research specifically to Domestic market.
22.	Sh. Satish Chandra	Group General Manager (Domestic)/ Corporate Office/ New Delhi	Incharge of Domestic business Marketing.
23.	Sh. Koushik Mukhopadhyaya	Group General Manager (Strategic Planning)/ Corporate Office/ New Delhi	Incharge of Strategic planning in Corporate Office
24.	Sh. M.K. Akhouri	Group General Manager (International Marketing)/ Corporate Office/ New Delhi	Incharge of marketing and business in the international segment
25.	Sh. Rajiv Rajvanshi	Group General Manager (Engg.)/ Corporate Office/ New Delhi	Incharge of Civil & Engg. Projects.
26.	Sh. N.L. Mankoja	Group General Manager (P&D)/ Corporate Office/ New Delhi	Incharge of Plainning & Development

...(Contd.)

S.No.	Name	Designation & Address	Duties
27.	Sh. Ajay Kumar	Group General Manager (Tech.)/ Corporate Office/ New Delhi	Incharge of Tech. Department. Department. Over-seeing procurement and maintaining of Wagons and other Equipments.
28.	Sh. R.S. Meena	Group General Manager (Comml.)/ Corporate Office/ New Delhi	Incharge of Commercial claims and other Commer-cial matters.
29.	Ms. Ameeta Suri	Group General Manager (Customs & Training)/ Corporate Office/ New Delhi	Incharge of Co-ordination with Customs, Training and Official Language Dept.
30.	Sh. Amit Chaudhri	Group General Manager (Operations & Shipping)/ Corporate Office/New Delhi	Incharge of CONCOR Rail Operations & Shipping
31.	Sh. Rajeev Bhardwaj	Sr. General Manager (HR)/ Corporate Office/ New Delhi	Incharge of HR Department

Organisational Pattern of CONCOR

- CONCOR is a company managed by its Board of Directors, constituted under the Companies Act, consisting of Government of India nominees and independent Directors.
- The day-to-day activities of CONCOR are managed under the leadership of the Board of Directors assisted by the in-charge of the respective departments.
- Detailed execution of the job is being done under the leadership of the in-charge of the respective departments.

Various Rules, Regulations, Instruction Manuals and Guidelines

- Corporate policy decision of running the businesses of CONCOR is being taken, depending upon the changing scenario of the Business by the Board of Directors.

- The day-to-day activities to be carried out are being decided by the respective departments and are being executed in conformity with the Corporate decision taken by CONCOR in the meeting of its Board of Directors.
- Since CONCOR is formed under the Companies Act, accordingly company is working within the purview of regulations framed in this regard by way of Memorandum and Articles of Association.

REFERENCES

1. *Human Resource Management* by VSP Rao—Excel Books, pp. 5-8
2. *Personnel Management* by CB Mamoria, Himalaya Publishing House, pp. 40-58.
3. *Indian Economy* by Dutt and Sundaram, Sultan Chand, New Delhi, p. 34-46.

Chapter 9

Findings and Conclusion

On the basis of studies on logistics management concepts following are the findings. Conceptually logistics is recently added as a jargon of integrated business management, the major functions of management like marketing, finance, production and personnel is considered a traditional field due to rapid change in the scope and wide use, logistics is defined as having the right quantity at the right time for the right price.

On the basis of various discussion following are important findings and conclusion of our study:

Role of Logistics Management in International and Domestic Trade

Logistics management has taken a center stage in Indian economy. In this globalised era where companies are working on rather thin margins it is additional pressure on them to reduce cost of production to be competitive in marketplace, the only way out is to focus on cost of logistics. Now-a-days due to metamorphosis of logistics scenario as a whole companies are able to save their money considerably.

Following are demand and supply drivers drawn from our study related to the recent practices in logistics management in international and domestic trade:

Demand Drivers

- Robust GDP and EXIM growth—Prospects of logistics industry are closely tied to the growth in GDP and Foreign Trade. GDP growth expected at ~6%, EXIM at 15-20%.
- Increased FDI Investment—Strong FDI flows in automotive, retail, capital goods, electronics and telecom to increase the need for logistics services.
- Increased outsourcing of logistics function—Companies to concentrate on their core activities to maintain competitiveness and outsource logistics function.

Supply Drivers

- Investment in Infrastructure—Government's planned outlay for development of roads, railway, ports and airports at US$80bn.
- Integrated service offerings by players—More and more logistics players are expanding their service offerings to provide complete logistics solutions.

Constraints

- Poor infrastructure facilities—Poor infrastructure results in slow movement of traffic and inefficiency. On an average a commercial vehicle in India runs at a speed of 20 miles per hour (mph) compared to over 60 mph in the Western Europe and the USA.
- Fragmented nature of the industry—The industry is very fragmented with existence of various small players. Lack of scale increases the cost of services for customers.
- Complex tax structure—Significant amount of time is spent in complying with inter state tax requirements and at transport check points, affecting the cost and competitiveness of both 3PL providers as well as their customers.

- The total transport function is shared among several actors. For example, operators perform only the haulage function, while the marketing, aggregating, storing and delivery functions are undertaken by agents and brokers.
- Non-time sensitive transportation services, cost is the key criteria.
- Industry growth rate estimated at 12-15% p.a. Express Logistics
- The core business of express industry is to provide door-to-door transportation of next day or time-definite shipments. Time definite shipments generally involve a transit time of 2-3 days.
- Express transportation is achieved by using a variety of transportation modes; trucks, vans, trains, passenger aircraft, freight aircraft as well as on-foot delivery. Though express companies prefer surface transport, air transportation is used in cases, where the transit time makes it impossible for goods to be delivered by surface transport.
- The size of Indian express industry was estimated at Rs 71 bn in 2006, which is nearly 1% the size of global express industry. The fastest growing industry in the logistics space. Estimated to have grown at 30%+ CAGR over the past decade. (*Source:* CARE)
- Organised segment constitutes 65% of the express market in India. Major players include Blue Dart, Gati and Overnite Express.

Role of CONCOR in Logistics Management of Country for the Enhancement of Rrade

Besides transportation, CONCOR provides a number of value added services like warehousing (both transit as well as bonded), less than container load (LCL) consolidation, custom clearance, factory stuffing and destuffing and container maintenance. The company recently made a foray in the cold chain business through its wholly owned subsidiary Fresh and Healthy Enterprises Ltd. (we have not factored the same in our projections). As of March 2007, it had a total base of 8,300 wagons (including wagons leased from the Indian Railways) and a network of 58 rail-linked terminals. CONCOR has established itself at the center place of managing logistics of any company. We understand and know it very clearly that the containerisation has a very important role to play in managing logistics and in this reference following are point of conclusions regarding the broad role played by CONCOR in enhancing international and domestic trade preceded by highlights of detailed analysis of CONCOR:

- Container logistics Market size estimated at Rs 100 bn is further bifurcated into: container haulage, CFS/ ICD services and MTO.
- Total container traffic handled at ports stood at 6.2 MM TEUs in FY07, with JNPT and Chennai together accounting for ~65% of the total cargo handled. Container traffic estimated to grow at 16% CAGR by 2012 to 13.0 MM TEUs by FY12.
- Containerised cargo represents 16% of the total cargo handled at major ports. The share of container traffic in non-bulk cargo is close to 47% in India, compared to 80% globally.
- 55% of the containerized cargo moved to/from ports through roads (rest by rail). Higher the distance, higher the share of share of rail in moving containers.
- National Maritime Development Board (NMDP) envisages investment of Rs560 Bn for increasing the container handling capacity at ports by nearly 3x by FY12.

Multimodal Transport Operator

- MTO's (Multimodal Transport Operator) Principal activities include consolidation and transportation of

LCL (less than container load) cargo, and full container load (FCL) forwarding using different modes of transport like sea, rail and road.

- Acts as a single point of contact for customers.
- Low capital intensive business as players hardly own any asset in the supply chain but instead rely on standalone service providers. CFS/ICD (Container Freight Station/Inland Container Depot). Both are custom bonded in-transit facilities with the only difference being CFS is located near the port, while an ICD is located in the hinterland.
- Key service offerings include container transportation to/from port (in case of CFS), stuffing/de-stuffing of container, general and bonded warehousing and customs clearance.
- Of the total containers handled at ports: ~35% of the traffic is destined for CFSs, ~65% for ICDs. Container Haulage. Haulage business relates to movement of containers between port and CFS/ICD. Movement between CFS and Port is always by road due to shorter distance involved. Movement between port and ICD can be either by road or rail.
- Asset intensive business (Sales/GFA of ~1.5x), with significant investments required in rolling stocks and land cost for ICDs.
- Despite new entrants, CONCOR continues to dominate the rail container haulage business. Real competition is from the road segment.

Financial Highlights

- While the volume growth for CONCOR has been strong at 16% YoY for 9MFY08 (last 10-Yr CAGR of 12%), realisations have witnessed a 6% YoY decline (last 10-Yr CAGR growth at 7%). This has resulted in a 9% YoY growth in top line, but a 2% YoY decline in EBITDA growth for the said period.

- We believe that decline in realisations in 1HFY08 was more or less an aberration. The reduction in realisations in the EXIM segment was led by passing on the benefit of reduction in haulage charges by Indian Railways and a cut in terminal handling charges on 40 ft containers. Also, due to mismatch between export and import traffic, the number of wagons running empty increased to 15% in Q2FY08. To increase the utilisatition of wagons, Concor deployed some of these wagons on the domestic segment, on which it had to offer discounts to attract traffic.
- We believe that long-term fundamentals of the company are intact and the decline in realisations is more or less transient in nature led by extra-ordinary situations rather than increase in competition. The same is substantiated by the improved 3QFY08 results, which witnessed a 3.4% QoQ increase in realisations. As a result, PBIT margins improved by 1.9% QoQ to 25.5%. Volume growth was also strong at 20% YoY (flat on a QoQ basis). The number of wagons running empty on the EXIM segment declined to 8% in the quarter. We expect CONCOR to report 14% CAGR in earnings between FY08-09 on the back of a 16% CAGR in sales.
- Long-term demand drivers intact over the last decade (FY97-07), Concor has witnessed a 12% CAGR in volumes, against an average GDP growth of 6.6% during the same period. This means, over a longer period of time, growth in container traffic for Concor is nearly 1.8x the GDP growth. Despite appreciation in the Indian rupee, the volume growth in the EXIM segment for 9MFY08 has been strong at 13.6% YoY (overall volume growth at 16.1% YoY). We expect Concor to register a 13% CAGR in volumes over FY08-10E, based on 1.6x our GDP growth estimate of 8%. According to Ministry of Shipping, the total

container traffic handled at ports is expected to register a 16% CAGR over FY07-12 to reach 13 MM TEUs.

- Concor to maintain leadership position in rail haulage Despite entrance of new players in the container rail movement, Concor has been able to maintain its leadership position with 90%+ market share. We are of the firm view that the new entrants will be unable to provide any meaningful competition to Concor, given their problems in procuring rolling stocks and building a rail-linked ICD network. Inability to absorb high cost of running empty wagons till the business reaches a critical mass will also prove to be a dampener. In fact, we have already seen some consolidation with new players teaming up with Concor for sharing of infrastructure. Higher return ratios combined with strong balance sheet Although rail haulage is a capital intensive business (Sales/ GFA of ~1.5x), the return ratios are quite attractive (ROE of ~25%, ROIC of ~30%). This combined with negative working capital (net of cash) requirements results in significant free cash flow to the firm (Rs 5.1 bn in FY07).
- The company is debt-free with significant amount of cash on books. Cash per share at the end of FY07 stood at Rs 210 per share and is expected to increase to Rs 328 per share by FY10 (19% of CMP).

Marketing Considerations in CONCOR

From its humble beginning in 1988, it is now an undisputed market leader having the largest network of 58 ICDs/CFSs in India. To sustain its market leadership CONCOR's marketing effort revolves around following questions:

1. What problems do the company's customers (potential customers) has that the offering (products or services) can solve better than those of other marketers).

2. What is the profile of the customer having this consumption problem?
3. What are the particular stages and circumstances (actual/potential).

These questions draw out attention of the research on the following important conclusions related to marketing efforts of CONCOR—

- Formulation of a sound service mix for the Indian Railways which make available to the user's world class goods traffic services.
- Promoting the services with the help of innovative measures to inform sense and persuade the users that they are offering the world calls services at a reasonable fare and freight structure.
- Offering promised services to the end users and bridging over the gap between the services-promised and services-offered.
- Rationalising the fair and freight structures so that the commercial viability is maintained.
- Developing quality personnel for the Indian Railways who are supposed to be personally committed and value-based.
- Adding additional attractions to the services so that the Indian Railways prove and continue to be number one.

Human Resource Philosophy and Beliefs

The fundamental objective of the HR in CONCOR is to provide the organisation with well-trained and well-motivated employees who will employ their skills and abilities effectively to help CONCOR achieve its goals and promote a sense of belongingness and harness retention of employees. The total employee strength in CONCOR is 1265(Executive cadre 265 and non-executive cadre: 1000) as on 31st March 2008 and to achieve employee satisfaction CONCOR HAS

INTRODUCED e-HR through information technology and it helps in taking care of the amount of remuneration to be paid to an employee for services rendered.

Remuneration Policy

CONCOR has a sound remuneration policy that helped it in (*a*) securing efficient personnel, (*b*) greater employee satisfaction and thereby (*c*) ensuring the achievement of organisational goals effectively.

The salient features of the compensation plan in CONCOR are as follows:[1]

(*a*) Wage and salary structure having two components namely "Basic Wage and Salary" and "Dearness Allowance" and some special pay allowance in high performance area.

(*b*) Inter unit disparities in the existing wage and salary structures including fringe benefits.

(*c*) An annual minimum bonus unrelated to profits and up to 20 percent if there are reasonable profits at the unit level.

(*d*) Provision of periodic wage revision (usually four years) namely on the basis of collective bargaining and more or less unrelated to profits, production and productivity.

Recruitment Policy of CONCOR

The basic tenets of CONCOR recruitment policy are summarised below:

1. Unskilled workers should be drawn from the locality when the project is situated.
2. Skilled workers, clerks and other non-technical staffs are recruited locally presided they fulfill the basic qualification.
3. Middle level Technical and Non-technical posts, having higher starting salaries equal to class I Junior

scale of the Government of India are to be filled by the principal criteria.

4. Higher Non-technical posts is filled from the candidates available in the industrial management pull failing which the post is advertised on all India basis.
5. Vacancies for unskilled labour clerk and other employees of low grades etc. is communicated to the employment exchange for the project.
6. All applications along with the list sent by the employment exchange is screened and appointments made by the selection committee of the CONCOR.
7. For the higher and medium level posts at least one representative of the Central Government official who is on the Board of Directors is included in the selection committee.

At last we can infer with full sense of responsibility that no case study is complete without SWOT analysis, so on the basis of findings of our research, following is the SWOT analysis of CONCOR:

Strengths

- Strong Infrastructure
- Backed and controlled by Indian Government
- None of the private operators can match in terms of rakes, terminals and most important, the size of trained manpower
- Virtual monopoly in its sector
- Steady financial performance

Weakness

- Bureaucratic structure
- Outdated transport technology
- Poor domestic marketing
- High maintenance cost

Opportunities

- Robust GDP and EXIM growth
- Increased FDI Investment
- Increased outsourcing of logistics function

Threats

- Competition from private container train operators
- Trigger of price war in recent future
- Three forth of Business concentrated mostly in western ports.

Suggestions

On the basis of facts and findings following are important suggestions of our research:

(1) CONCOR must ensure that the existing capacity is effectively maintained and that such maintenance is provided for and that provisions so made are in fact used for the purpose.

(2) To maximise the utilisation of the existing assets through higher productivity to be achieved through technological improvements as also more efficient management and operation.

(3) To promote multi-modal transport operation through introduction of modernised container services.

(4) To have a cost based price structure and to improve the financial viability of load factor of containers.

(5) CONCOR should examine profitable freight routes and identify the new demand areas and bottlenecks in the freight transport routes, where railway lines are required to be in place to connect import/export gateways.

(6) CONCOR should broaden the use of double stack containers under the electric wire routes to capture the car transportation market in the country by

moving almost double the number of cars per train against the present capacity.

(7) To encourage domestic container traffic CONCOR should initiate its effort as available figures confirm that the volume of domestic container traffic is negligible compared to international traffic.

(8) To reduce the unit cost of transportation triple stack containers of smaller sizes on domestic routes be used for higher volumes of relatively lightweight and high value cargo such as automobile parts, electronics and electrical components, readymade garments, tea, medicinal items, spices, plastic goods, jute, leather goods, de-oiled cakes and paper, in each rake.

(9) To keep its effective presence in the domestic sector company should encourage domestic marketing not restricted to industrial users only.

(10) To use more innovative practices in order to maintain its position as the opening of the sector has brought private players in the competition.

(11) To make a remarkable improvement in operating efficiency of rake management system, freight transportation, terminal management, enquiry system etc. Information Technology should be implemented extensively.

Bibliography

Books

1. *The Management of Business Logistics—A Supply Chain Perspective* by Coyle, Bardi, Langley-Thompson Press, 2007, p. 36-52
2. Vrat, P., 1999. *Supply Chain Management in India: Problems and Challenges,* Vikas Publishing, New Delhi.
3. *Containerisation, Multimodal Transport and Infrastructure Development in India* by Dr KV Hariharan, Shroff Publication, New Delhi 2005.
4. *A Textbook on Container and Multimodal Transport Management* by Dr. KV Hariharan, Shroff Publication, New Delhi 2005.
5. *Containerisation and Multimodal Transport in India* by Dr. KV Hariharan, Shroff Publication, New Delhi, 2005.
6. Raghuram, G. and N. Rangaraj (eds) *Logistics and Supply Chain Management: Concept and Cases,* Macmillan, 2008.
7. *Laws of Carriage of Goods* by Dr. KV Hariharan, Shroff Publication, 2006, New Delhi.
8. *Logistics Management—Supply Chain Imperative* by Vinod Sople, Pearson Education Publication, New Delhi, 2006.
9. Ravi Babu, M.A. *Disaggregate Study of Mode of Choice for Inland Movement of Export Cargo. Containerized on Marine Segment,* IIM, Ahemadabad, 2001.
10. Ravi Babu, M.A. *Disaggregate Study of Mode of Choice for Inland Movement of Export Cargo. Containerised on Marine Segment,* FPM Thesis, IIM, Ahemadabad, 2001.

11. *Nabhi's Exporters Manual and Documentation*—2007, A Nabhi Publication, New Delhi.
12. *International Marketing—Analysis and Strategy* by Sak Onkvisit, John J. Shaw Prentice Hall of India Publication, New Delhi, 2005
13. *Export Marketing* by Cherian and Parab, Himalaya Publishing House, New Delhi, 2007.
14. *Textbook of Logistics and Supply Chain Management* by DK Agrawal, Macmillan, New Delhi.
15. *Logistics Management and World Seaborne Trade* by Krishnaveni Muthiah, Himalaya Publishing House 2008.
16. *Marketing Management* by Philip Kotler (Eleventh Edition) ; Prentice Hall of India, New Delhi, 2005.
17. Govt of India : *Handbook of Procedures, Import and Export Promotion,* New Delhi, 2007.
18. *Logistics Management*-K. Shridhara Bhatt, Himalaya Publishing House., New Delhi, 2007.
19. *Logistics Management* -K. Shridhara Bhatt, Himalaya Publishing House, New Delhi, 2006.
20. *Financial Management* by I.M. Pandey, Vikas Publishing, New Delhi, 2006.
21. *Methodology of Research in Social Sciences* by OR Krishnaswami & M.Ranganatham, Himalaya Publishing House, New Delhi, 2006.
22. *Financial Statement Analysis*—The ICFAI University Press, Hyderabad, ICFAI Publication, Hyderabad, 2007.
23. *Financial Accounting—A Managerial Perspective* by R. Narayanaswami-Prentice Hall of India, New Delhi, 2006.
24. *Logistics Management* by Reji Ismail-Excel Books, New Delhi, 2005.
25. *Transportation Infrastructure Engineering* by Hoel, Lester, Nicholas J., Prentice Hall Of India, New Delhi, 2006.
26. *Human Resource Management* by VSP Rao-Excel Books., New Delhi, 2006.
27. *Statistical Methods* by SP Gupta—Sultan Chand Books, New Delhi, 2005.
28. *UP Export Corporation Limited Handbook* (A Govt. of UP undertaking) Kanpur, India, 2004.

Journals

1. Rangaraj, Narayan and AK Srivastava, *Some IT Imperatives for Indian Railways in a Supply Chain Management (on) National Connectivity Vision,* Surface Transportation and Communication, Indian National Academy of Engineering, Secunderabad, January, 2001.
2. Rangaraj, N.and N.Vishwanadham, *Multimodal Containerised Transport for Export and Import Through Western India*–a Supply Chain perspective, Technical Report, The Logistics Institute-Asia Pacific, National University and Indian Institute of Technology, Bombay, India, 2001.
3. *Cargo Times* Vol. 3, issue 4, June 2006.
4. *Cargo Times* Vol. 7, issue, 3, June 2007.
5. *Logistics Management*–Indian Edition by Reed Infomedia India, Vol. 1, issue 1, April 2007.
6. *Logistics Management*–Indian Edition by Reed Infomedia India, Vol. 2, issue 1, April 2008.
7. *Logistics Management*–Indian Edition by Reed Infomedia India, Vol. 2, issue 4, July 08.
8. *Logistics Management*–Indian Edition by Reed Infomedia India, Vol. 2, issue 5, August, 2008.

Annual Reports

1. *Survey of Indian Industry 2005*–The Annual Hindu Publication, The Hindu Group of Publication, Chennai.
2. *Survey of Indian Industry 2006*–The Annual Hindu Publication, The Hindu Group of Publication, Chennai.
3. *Survey of Indian Industry 2007*–The Annual Hindu Publication, The Hindu Group of Publication, Chennai.
4. Rastogi, A.(2006) *"Indian Infrastructure Report,"* Oxford University Press, 9-12, New Delhi.
5. *Annual Reports of CONCOR,* published by CONCOR 2002-07.
6. *Hand Book on Multimodal Transport (Containerisation) and Logistics Management,* Institute Of Rail Transport, New Delhi, 2004.

Newspapers

1. Bhatt, N. (2006)" CONCOR-Sailing Through", *Business Standard,* 8 Sept, 2006.

2. Rastogi, A.(2006) *"Indian Infrastructure Report"*, Oxford University Press, 9-12.
3. Sanjeevi, (2003) "Logistics in a Competitive Milieu" *The Hindu*, 23 December 2006.
4. Srinivasan, G(2006) "Public-Private Partnership is the Way to Build Infrastructure", *Hindu Business Line*, 7 October 2007.
5. Acharya, R.C. "Railways Heavy Task", *Economic Times,* 20 Nov., 2007.
6. Logistics: The Next Big Growth Driver, article by V. Shunmugum and Ritambhara Singh–*Business Line*, Saturday, March 29, 2008, p. 8.

Websites

1. www.wikipaedia.org
2. www.indianrail.gov.in
3. www.economywatch.com
4. www.etintelligence.com
5. www.gati.com
6. www.indianseaport.com
7. www.concorindia.com

Index